Critical Thinking in Counselling and Psychotherapy

Critical Thinking in Counselling and Psychotherapy

Colin Feltham

Los Angeles | London | New Delhi
Singapore | Washington DC

SAGE Publications Ltd
1 Oliver's Yard
55 City Road
London EC1Y 1SP

SAGE Publications Inc.
2455 Teller Road
Thousand Oaks, California 91320

SAGE Publications India Pvt Ltd
B 1/I 1 Mohan Cooperative Industrial Area
Mathura Road
New Delhi 110 044

SAGE Publications Asia-Pacific Pte Ltd
33 Pekin Street #02-01
Far East Square
Singapore 048763

Library of Congress Control Number: 2009940508

British Library Cataloguing in Publication data

A catalogue record for this book is available from the British Library

ISBN 978-1-84860-018-8
ISBN 978-1-84860-019-5 (pbk)

Typeset by C&M Digitals (P) Ltd, Chennai, India
Printed by CPI Antony Rowe, Chippenham, Wiltshire
Printed on paper from sustainable resources

Contents

Acknowledgements

I would like to thank Alice Oven very warmly for her enthusiasm, guidance and hands-on help at critical stages in this book's progress.

What Is Critical Thinking?

What critical thinking isn't

An easy, 'official' answer can be given to the first question, and I will supply a version of it, but it is necessary first to prepare the ground by stating a view on what critical thinking is not and to offer an argument for it being something counsellors might benefit from being more interested in. At the same time, I want to establish a case here for a certain kind of critical thinking that is subject-specific, that has embedded within it some core values of honesty.

The word 'critical' is naturally associated with negative criticism, and particularly in the counselling and therapy field with parental criticism. The concept of *Critical Parent* found in transactional analysis (TA) reminds us that one of the components of adult distress is often the damaging negative injunctions passed on from parents to children: 'You mustn't be like this or act in this way, you must be more like me, you're always doing such and such, why can't you be normal?' Along with the person-centred tradition's emphasis on conditions of worth as a major cause of adult distress, this TA concept has probably been highly influential in making all in the therapy world sensitive to anything critical that smacks of judgementalism and negativity, of non-acceptance and undermining. Perhaps these combine too with a general social climate of well-intentioned 'political correctness' and intellectual postmodernism that emphasize difference and diversity and de-emphasize the possibility of any critical position based largely on rationality. Counselling has naturally mistrusted an over-emphasis on intellectualization, and even in an academic training context there is some ambivalence about the usefulness of philosophical, analytical and scientific perspectives on human distress, human relationships and how to help make improvements.

Critical thinking, especially in an educational context (Cottrell, 2005), may also sometimes be associated with difficult and useless abstract analysis and with pedantry. I think there is some justice in this suspicion. Mainstream education probably does have a tendency to over-emphasize and fetishize the value of intellectual criticism and textual micro-analysis. Perhaps originally there were good reasons to promote a highly analytical attitude but this then became a tradition that can be oppressive, that can unintentionally kill rather than foster curiosity. We know that many students begin to study psychology with an enthusiastic expectation of understanding more about human nature, for example, yet often become disillusioned when they find themselves compelled to study animal behaviour, statistics, the various preoccupations of 'dead white males' and so on.

On the related matter of pedantry, take the following example. Pedantically, I can get a little critically obsessed with the habit some have of referring to couple counselling as *couples* counselling. I see no justification for this latter usage (after all, no-one refers to individuals counselling or to groups or families counselling) and I consider it an ugly and incorrect term. But such obsessional pedantry is hardly productive. In other words, it's not 'critical', it's somewhat trivial in this case. But it is important (I think) to ask about the meaning and value of couple counselling: is 'the relationship' the client? Does it work? Is it based on outdated, heterosexist, couplist and Western assumptions? These are important questions. Similarly, we can either accept that a phenomenon such as sex addiction is real, or we may apply critical thinking to questions about social assumptions (and our own prejudices) about sexuality.

Critical thinking is naturally sceptical, not taking statements at face value. But there are at least two areas in which we might need to rein it in. First, on pragmatic grounds, we cannot make any progress sometimes unless we take some things for granted or temporarily suspend possible objections. For example, if you read again what you've read above, and read it all critically, analysing each statement, you will find me making certain assumptions or failing to supply evidence. But I believe the text would rapidly become too self-conscious, complicated and dry if I did this. Second, but closely related, if critical thinking becomes dominant and obsessive it can lead to a kind of nihilism, a philosophical and often emotional attitude in which nothing is held to be of any value and despair can take over. I don't think there is any formula to tell us exactly when to be more pragmatic than critical or when enough critical thinking is enough. But we need to remain cautious about these pulls. Or do we? Remember, my statement 'we need to remain cautious' is only *my* conclusion at a certain time and place, and is in fact associated with my own philosophical limitations, personal temperament and professional anxieties. Later in this book I do at times move towards instances of deep and analytical thinking that may not be pragmatic or practical.

I hope to show by the many examples given throughout the book that critical thinking is relevant to everyday counselling practice, to its training and development. It is not intended as an exercise in empty cleverness and it will have failed if it is widely perceived as a text detached from raw counselling issues. Too many critical thinking texts focus atomistically on detailed textual analysis instead of an analysis of practice and profession. If there is a single (or two-part) critical question that drives my own thinking and to some extent underpins this book, for me it is 'Why do we human beings suffer and how can we best and most honestly address it?' For me, and I hope for readers, this question is far more important than, say, 'How can I fill in my accreditation forms?' or 'How many hours of supervision should we have?' A wide variety of questions may be raised in the counselling arena but arguably some are much more fundamental and pervasive than others. Close critical-analytical reading of texts is important but 'wide angle' reading, interpretation and vision and 'blue-skies thinking' are important too.

Why counsellors need to engage in critical thinking

We seem to accept that counselling, psychotherapy and cognate disciplines should be taught in or validated by colleges and universities, part of whose remit has always been to promote a certain critical-analytical tradition and to insist on what is called evidence instead of – or as well as – an uncritically subjective belief. We tacitly accept that there is some dividing line between what should and should not be taught in further and higher education. I have heard few counsellors, for example, arguing that astrology or scientology should be incorporated into mainstream education. So I suspect that most of us have some implicit sense of the value of locating counselling training in colleges and universities. However impassioned we may be about our chosen or preferred model of counselling – and of course many of our models promote an emphasis on feelings, spirituality and the body that isn't found elsewhere in mainstream education – we seem to recognize that they must be exposed to some degree of critical analysis and rational discussion. We may not call it critical thinking but it is already, implicitly, something of that sort.

Another recommendation for critical thinking is this – that it has in fact been highly influential in shaping the field of counselling and psychotherapy. Critical reflection on Freud's views spurred Jung and Adler to move away from classical Freudian assumptions and create their own models, and the development of psychotherapy is characterized by similar conceptual disagreements throughout its history. Carl Rogers was critical of prevailing psychoanalytic and behavioural models; Aaron Beck and Albert Ellis both rejected their own psychoanalytic backgrounds as part of developing their own forms of cognitive behavioural therapy (CBT); and so on. In other words, a critical attitude towards existing traditions underpins the very fabric of counselling and psychotherapy. This critical thinking also drives daily creativity in practice, in clinical reasoning (Pesut & Herman, 1999). Skovholt and Ronnestad's (1995: 110) classic study of therapists' professional development noted a significant 'movement from received knowledge toward constructed knowledge'.

Perhaps at this point you may agree that we tend to welcome criticism of traditions and assumptions that we subjectively dislike but we are less inclined to analyse critically our own cherished traditions and assumptions. For example, you may dislike the government's evidence-based trend in psychotherapy and counselling in a healthcare context and be enthusiastic about opposing it, but simultaneously oppose any criticism of your own allegiance to psychodynamic, humanistic or cognitive-behavioural theory and practice.

I have an interesting caveat here, and it accompanies what I have said above about pragmatism and nihilism. One of the great strengths of counselling is its focus on what undermines positive or optimal mental health or, put differently, its sensitivity to pathological trends and drives. One everyday and clinical observation is that some of us suffer from too much self-doubt, from thinking too much, often obsessively, and from an inability to make decisions and commitments. A defence mechanism for some of us is to be overly analytical. There is a certain kind of clever suspicion of beliefs that may be associated with adolescent rebelliousness, an obverse of the Critical Parent, a reactive opposition to anything that seems authoritarian. An accompaniment to depression is often the belief that nothing has any ultimate substance. Again, I have no formula for avoiding these problems but simply issue a caution here. We could argue that a commitment to singular models of counselling is a sign of healthy attachment *or* a feature of intellectual weakness and insecurity. We might say that eclecticism reflects a splintered, butterfly mind *or* a healthy flexibility. We can argue that being too interested in our clients' early life events, or in their sexuality or spirituality, is unwise, but that an avoidance of such considerations is also unwise. I suspect that we all need to hold many such questions in mind as critical alternatives. Most counsellors will know that in everyday practice this is exactly what they do – follow certain paths of reflection with their clients while mentally bracketing other hypotheses for later consideration.

Another argument for critical thinking is simply that many of us suffer (and I personally think this a probability rather than a possibility) from *not thinking* and *not even allowing ourselves to think* about aspects of our distress, confusion or unhappiness. While some of us think too much, others think too little. Some of us emotionalize or 'think emotionally' so that we cannot get a close conceptual grip on what troubles us and whence it originates. Traumatic events or chronic habits sometimes shut down or distort our ability to think clearly about our personal problems; this is territory well covered by cognitive therapy. But I believe most of us severely limit the scope of our thinking about the kind of society we have to live in, the history of our species, human nature itself, and how all of this impacts on us personally, especially on our mental health. Counselling is understandably dominated by theories about individuals, what goes on in their families and in their minds, and how to help them. The psychological therapies generally are not concerned with, or at best make tentative noises towards, the 'social contexts' of mental distress; and clients, likewise, are often befuddled by assumptions and often feel guilty or ignorant about the origins of distress. However well-intentioned the field of counselling is, it is possible that its analysis of the aetiology of distress is limited or incorrect. Hence, critical thinking must embrace the contexts in which we come to suffer.

What is critical thinking?

I hope it is already becoming apparent what I mean by critical thinking and especially by critical thinking in the context of counselling and therapy (in its theory, training, supervision, everyday practice, research and professional structures). I will now turn to spell this out more explicitly and outline some links with other traditions that feed into our current focus.

Strangely, many conventional texts on critical thinking largely ignore its obvious roots in ancient Greek philosophy, for example in the well-known analytical and dialogical style of Socrates and his readiness to stand by his conclusions and even to die for them. Philosophy since then has taken on both the big questions of existence itself and the endless micro-analyses of language that too easily deceive us. Meanwhile, human beings have invested hope and a belief in religion and sought evidence in the natural world through science. Arguably, the psychotherapeutic tradition has been propelled by much hope and belief but has only fairly recently pursued 'hard' evidence.

Philosophical tools have been used in cognitive therapy (from the original stoical thought of Epictetus) and in existential therapy stemming from nineteenth-century philosophers. Foucault, Lacan and others have applied linguistic, philosophical and socio-political critiques that have led to new perspectives in therapy (Loewenthal, 2003). These have all underpinned hypotheses and clinical reasoning. Indeed Ellenberger (1971) locates the roots of much 'dynamic psychiatry' in the ancient Greek schools of philosophy. A return to critical 'philosophical' thinking in contemporary psychological therapies may be long overdue.

Fisher (2001) gathers together a number of definitions of contemporary methodical critical thinking. Recurring terms are persistent effort, careful consideration, thoughtful, logical enquiry, careful reasoning, skilfulness, evidence-seeking, reflective thinking, preparation for decision making, evaluation of arguments. These are applied generically, in other words to many settings, whether you are faced with buying a used car, judging the impartiality of a news item, voting for a particular politician or assessing the merits of a course textbook. Fisher also commends *critico-creative thinking*, that is, critique that leads to new ways of thinking and practice. Cottrell (2005: 2) describes critical thinking as a 'complex process of deliberation which involves a wide range of skills and attitudes'. Her given components include scepticism (or 'polite doubt'), an analysis of how arguments are constructed, an awareness of one's own reasons and realistic self-appraisal, underlying thinking skills and knowledge and research. Identifying positions and arguments, evaluating evidence, considering alternative arguments, reading between the lines, identifying false assumptions, using logic and insight and being able to draw conclusions are all parts of the process.

To some extent we are all skilled in critical assessment, whether by birth (animals assess their surroundings continuously for nourishment and threat) or learning. But we are vulnerable to bias and misjudgement, to being deceived; we all have some weaknesses in our ability to evaluate dispassionately and comprehensively, and probably we can all improve our critical thinking. Clearly critical thinking requires a pre-existing ability to think and to apply somewhat patiently an analytical method. Intellectual disability will limit our critical thinking but so too will mental ill health (whether temporary or chronic), dogmatism, implicit prejudices and some learning styles. Sometimes counsellors object that their best work is based on intuition or a gut instinct that cannot be explained, and there is probably some truth in this. But intuition is often composed of very rapid, subliminal critical assessment and decision-making processes rather than their absence, and our gut instinct can certainly be wrong. An explicit consideration of some of the principles of critical thinking stands a good chance of improving our thinking and educating our intuition.

Conversely, however, impatient passion also has its place, especially in the culture of therapy, in the intense relationship with suffering individuals, especially in a society that often suppresses emotion in favour of ritualized social interaction. Therapists have to hold such tensions.

That being said, I suggest that a working definition of critical thinking for the purposes of this book might be:

> The willingness to approach all relevant traditions, practices, texts and questions sceptically and analytically, with an associated effort to articulate the grounds for criticism and to make possible alternative proposals.

This definition cannot tell us what level of critique we might bring to bear. Critical thinking itself can opt to remain safely academic – a mere exercise in clever observation – and relatively uncritical towards questions of social structure and how we ourselves might be implicated in oppressive structures and practices that cause distress. Crudely speaking, I think we must posit at least three kinds and levels of critical thinking: (1) critical thinking of a somewhat formulaic and arguably superficial, detached kind that we may be obliged to engage in for the sake of satisfying academic requirements; (2) critical thinking that may issue from a personal idiosyncrasy or intellectual commitment that has no significant impact on that which it critiques (in our case counselling and therapy); and (3) critical thinking that might fundamentally change oneself or raise the possibility of those engaged in radical critical dialogue changing, or institutional assumptions and practices being significantly changed. We might note too that critical thinking here includes aspects of thinking critically about practice, texts, professional discourse and associated moral, social and philosophical questions.

The context of critical thinking in the milieu of therapy

From the outset, psychoanalysis attracted criticism (Szasz, 1976) on many grounds and has received fierce critical focus from psychologists (Dawes, 1996; Eysenck, 1952; Rose, 1989; Smail, 2005), philosophers (Erwin, 1997) and others (Crews, 1999). Similarly, humanistic therapies have been attacked for their perceived naïvety, narcissism (Clare & Thompson, 1981; Weatherill, 2004), and cognitive behavioural models for their mechanistic and scientistic character (House & Loewenthal, 2008). More generally the psychotherapeutic field has been questioned on grounds of effectiveness, grandiosity, a perversion of commonsense values, political ignorance, amorality, as patriarchally uncritical, and having an anti-psychiatric (or pro-psychiatric) and anti-scientific attitude (Cloud, 1998; Dryden & Feltham, 1992; Furedi, 2004; Hillman & Ventura, 1992; Howard, 1996; Parker, 1999, 2007). Lynch (1996) regards psychoanalysis, for example, as no better or worse than Christianity or astrology in terms of being merely memetically self-reproducing. One of the most acute contemporary targets for critique is the professionalization of the field, regarded by many as anathema (Postle, 2007).

Some critics target specific therapies for their ire, others dismiss the entire edifice of therapy, and yet others simply regard psychotherapy as no more nor less 'fair game' for deconstruction than any other modern ideology. Yet others offer friendly insider criticism (Feltham, 1999a). My own critical oeuvre has sought to question a range of problems in psychotherapy (Dryden & Feltham, 1992; Feltham, 1999b); the identity of counselling (Feltham, 1995); the proliferation of and conflicts between approaches (Feltham, 1997); the assumptions underlying supervision (Lawton & Feltham, 2000); and much larger questions about the human condition (Feltham, 2007). For some, the further these topics move from a narrow clinical and professional focus, the less relevant they seem. For those like myself, there is a belief that we cannot make honest, fundamental progress without addressing these larger questions.

Finally let us reassert the point that counselling and psychotherapy represent a critique of society, or particularly of those social trends and institutions that are dehumanizing. Therapy and its linked concerns for emotional intelligence and good social relations highlight the damage done to children, the vulnerable, and indeed to all of us, by thoughtless brutal traditions. Most obviously therapy emphasizes the value of the individual and individual needs in mass society.

Which particular form of critical thinking best improves counselling?

Critical thinking has become something like an identified, bankable academic product. In other words, it has settled into a recognizable shape as a sub-discipline in its own right, offered as a generic skill, indeed as an AS level examination subject in the UK. Hopefully this trend has some good in it. But most things that become part of status quo education eventually lose their innovative edge, indeed we might say their critical edge. Critical *thinking* does, of course, commend thinking, and tends to imply – like cognitive therapy – that feelings are somehow less reliable than thinking and that the latter will correct the faults of the former. In counselling we can often see the limitations of this view. Yet a term like 'critical feelings' will not work, nor will 'critical emotion'. 'Critical being' comes closer perhaps (Barnett, 1997). Psychology has an internally critical group who refer to their endeavours as critical psychology (Fox & Prilleltensky, 1997; Parker, 2007; Sloan, 2000), and to some small extent the term 'critical counselling studies' may function similarly in counselling. It may be that no best term exists.

What I hope to achieve in this book is a recognition that counsellors can draw from the strengths of their concern for human distress and aspiration and their understanding of the nuances of subjectivity, while at the same time refusing to settle for outdated or counterproductive theories of counselling or an overly narrow mission for individual counselling. To some extent therapists have already shown their openness to a fruitful self-criticism in terms of micropractice issues (e.g. Dryden, 1992; Kottler, 2002; Robertiello & Schoenewolf, 1987). A critico-creative approach leads not simply to new techniques but also potentially to a radical analysis of the human condition and an allied consciousness-raising that might address suffering with powerful new ideas and actions.

Finke and Bettle (1996) use the term 'chaotic cognition' to value such a creative process. Brown and Rutter (2006) advocate critical thinking in social work, Groopman (2008) in medicine and Pesut and Herman (1999) in nursing and healthcare. Lavery (2007) shows how much religion in its mature forms has to benefit from critical assessment. Nelson-Jones (1989) has advocated the explicit teaching of better thinking skills for therapeutic purposes; Jackins (1978), the founder of re-evaluation co-counselling, advocated 'thinking all the time' as a therapeutic force, just as Holmes (2002) reflects on the importance of thinking within therapy itself; and Jacobs (2000) brings a specifically psychodynamic perspective to bear on thinking. While these are not all 'critical thinking' as such, taken together they do show what value sceptical, innovative, corrective and therapeutic thinking can have.

A brief guide to thinking critically about counselling texts

1 Try to articulate your own assumptions and their origins.
2 Approach all texts somewhat sceptically. Relevant texts include the classic 'bibles' of counselling and psychotherapy, e.g. *The Interpretation of Dreams, Client-Centered Therapy, Reason and Emotion in Psychotherapy*, etc.; but also explore texts by interpreters and translators of those texts and by writers and editors of anthologies of different therapeutic traditions.

3   Distortions, inaccuracies and outright errors can creep into the writing process. How did the authors come to their conclusions? What fallacies, ethnocentric assumptions, anachronisms and so forth might be perpetuated in these texts?

4   Case studies – how can you know how 'true' they are, or even whether they actually ever happened?

5   Technical and skills guides – how do you know these are really clinically road-tested and/or evidence-based, reliable skills?

6   Professional body documents – who wrote them, with what authority, for what purposes, with what possible political bias?

7   Research papers – how significant is the topic, as opposed to trivial? How sound and meaningful is the methodology? How much do the research findings improve on commonsense expectations?

8   How swayed are you by the reputations of authors and perhaps your own low self-esteem in relation to challenging them?

9   When writing assignments, case studies or other documents that require you to interpret published texts and theories, how fair, liberal or dogmatic do you find tutors and assessors?

10 How accessible and logical are texts, as opposed to being dense, unnecessarily complex, or full of exotic or obfuscating jargon?

11 Think also about your own limitations of vocabulary, comprehension and willingness to work at understanding.

12 Consider whether an appeal is being made on *logical* grounds (a rational, philosophical argument); on a formal *empirical* basis (research); on grounds of naturalistic *observation* and anecdote; or on grounds of *subjective introspection*. None of these is invalid and none is beyond critique, but often one party or another will assert their superiority.

13 Try to move away from a close analytical reading of texts to wider socio-political and philosophical perspectives on therapy as a contemporary constructed phenomenon, and then go back again.

In Appendix 1 an example is given of critical textual analysis, also called 'close reading'. By contrast, Appendix 2 lists items closer to practice, for an exercise in critical consideration. Appendix 3 then lists further questions to which critical thinking in the field of therapy may be applied. Case studies are given at the conclusion of each of the nine sections to encourage engagement in the relevant issues.

Reading and critiquing this book

I suggest you read this book as you see fit, for example dipping into and selecting those sections which particularly interest you. When reading, you might notice some things which make you angry or puzzled or bored. Are there any you violently disagree with? You might think some of the writing inadequate, confusing or clichéd. Have I pretended to possess knowledge when I merely have an opinion? Am I using too much anecdotal evidence, considered by some scholars to be illegitimate? Are there sections where I am writing illogically or emotionally, or over-intellectualizing? Am I being contrarian, polemical merely for the sake of it? Is there any point where I'm going too far, perhaps betraying counselling traditions by being too critical? Can one be too critical? Have I inadvertently made inaccurate statements?

I tend to think in terms of safe, conservative (uncritical) thinking; conservative critical thinking (similar to 'textbook critical thinking'); and radically critical thinking – and sometimes I am drawn to the latter. I am also attracted to the idea of radical honesty (Blanton, 1994). But what bias or psychopathology might be concealed within apparently unusual honesty? Similarly, what pathological bias could underpin those obscure academic writings that many of us simply cannot access? Please consider what rings true for you and what is helpful or otherwise. I have avoided presenting a formulaic 'How to think critically' book in favour of giving many examples of counselling-related topics that I have approached critically. I do not claim that my treatment of these topics is itself above critical reproach. I have grouped a number of sections under convenient headings but some may seem arbitrarily positioned. I have avoided the habit of saturating the text with academic references but have included some selected suggestions for further reading. I have followed my own interests in the choice of topics but have also tried to represent what I consider to be key issues for counsellors, trainers, supervisors and others. Again, the reader can (and perhaps should) reflect on what I have, inadvertently or otherwise, omitted from my selection.

NOTE Given the well-known and topical problem of distinguishing counselling from psychotherapy, rather than constantly repeating both terms or attempting to show tiny alleged differences, I have varied the terms in this text and often simply used 'counselling'. A fuller discussion can be found in Feltham (1995).

Everyday Counselling Practice

What Are the Pros and Cons of Unconditional Positive Regard?

The term 'unconditional positive regard' (UPR) was coined by Carl Rogers and equates with a deep acceptance of the client. Sometimes it is referred to as warmth, non-judgementalism and prizing. It is asserted that no effective counselling can take place without such acceptance, since a counsellor who overtly or covertly transmits their judgement or rejection is reinforcing exactly those negative experiences that others, such as parents, have been responsible for; and no successful counselling is likely to happen in a non-accepting relationship. The 'U' in the UPR connotes an ability to rise above typical social values and prejudices but it is often said that one does not have to approve of all a client's actions and attitudes – rather UPR means that you positively accept him as a person, perhaps sometimes bracketing off his more offensive features or understanding them as part of his best efforts to survive within difficult conditions. Sometimes it is said that UPR resembles the highest Christian form of love or *agape* (a pure concern for others, not based on any moral evaluation). As many religious adherents know, such love and also forgiveness can be extremely powerful, particularly for those who have known very little love or decency in their lives.

When asked at interview whether they have any difficulties with any individuals or groups of people, most candidates for training say something like this: 'No, I get on with everyone, I accept all kinds of people, I have worked in many multicultural settings'. UPR is thus conflated with a 'politically correct' attitude of celebrating diversity, having no conscious prejudices and actively striving to reduce or eliminate any residual ones. It can be too easily taken for granted from the outset that applicants for counselling training do not suffer from judgementalism and do not need much work on fostering UPR. Rigorous person-centred counsellors will insist that UPR is not a superficial attribute, does not come automatically or easily and requires disciplined personal development work.

The clearest area in which trainees will declare some difficulties is paedophilia. 'I could not work with paedophiles' is quite a common admission. This may be followed closely by rapists and hardcore racists. Paedophilia is often seen as beyond the pale, as impossible to understand or even to try to understand or forgive, as if such an attempt almost condones the paedophilia or lessens its seriousness. Then there is the attempt to suggest that one could accept the person of the paedophile but not his actions. Fundamentally, the paedophile, like everyone else, is 'good' but has met some challenging life circumstances that have set him on the wrong path. If he experiences UPR, combined with persistent empathy, then in theory he should be able to confront his own actions, accept his own 'pre-paedophilic' self, forgive himself and cease his paedophilia. But paedophilia, like drug addiction, is a hardened condition, frequently with a poor prognosis for positive change. Many trainees and practitioners instinctively know this and will thus avoid such work, and perhaps also feel that they might be contaminated by working with paedophiles. UPR in these circumstances may seem impossible. But others, with a strong faith in human beings, will believe that even the paedophile deserves profound human consideration, or deserves the effort to be contacted at a relational depth. Some counsellors might try to distinguish between paedophiles (or rapists) who are motivated and unmotivated for change.

What other difficulties are encountered in experiencing and offering UPR? Obviously, many will feel challenged by those who are openly racist, misogynistic, homophobic and disablist. It is possible to think and even declare, 'I do not like your racism (or other anti-social attitude) but I fully accept you as a person'. But things are seldom so straightforward. Such attitudes are often mixed up with personality nuances, incongruence and countertransference. Some people are more likeable than others, whatever their 'failings' or negative attitudes. Some counsellors are themselves not naturally very warm or forgiving, or may have idiosyncratic resistances and reactions to others' foibles. It seems likely that those with a natural openness will find UPR much easier. But it doesn't necessarily follow that openness is always accompanied by an ability for active empathy, or technical creativity or imaginative therapeutic work. It's possible that a highly conscientious and intelligent counsellor may have to work hard at certain aspects of UPR if, say, he comes from a family or culture in which he learned to be judgemental. UPR may be of a bland kind ('I get on with everyone') or of a profound nature. One strong philosophical justification for UPR is that we are all a mixture of 'good' and 'bad' features and that inside each of us there are remnants of dysfunctional and unloving attitudes and behaviour. Perhaps the luckier ones, with loving parents, a supportive and healthy environment and good genes, largely escaped the need to struggle with problematic and socially repellent behaviours. It can be said (indeed there are Christian precedents for saying) that sinners (or those most obviously antisocial) are most in need of love, or UPR.

Congruence can also seem to be at odds with UPR. At one level I accept, or strive to fully accept, my client. But at another I may have feelings that I cannot deny I have, of anger or irritation, unease or rejection towards my client. I have to decide whether, and when and how, to voice these feelings. Radical honesty as a human being, or a pressure for congruence within therapy, sometimes compels us to tell the other person that we object to their attitude, their language, views, poor hygiene or whatever. We may strive to 'say it nicely' but sometimes it will be experienced as rejecting or conditional. We may be able to work through such difficult moments successfully and sometimes they can even strengthen the therapeutic bond. Sometimes however they will not.

It looks likely that there are shades of UPR, including the somewhat false variety (the superficial 'portrayal' of UPR) at one end of a spectrum and a profound, perhaps spiritual quality of tender UPR at the other. There may be moments when the client might benefit from some straight talking about his or her obnoxious or self-defeating behaviour, when we ought to put aside any pretence of UPR (for example, 'It makes me shudder when you talk about your wife in that hateful and dismissive way'). Psychoanalysts might object that too strong or obvious an experience for the client of UPR might distort her unconscious feelings or their expression, just as some CBT writers have cautioned that too warm an acceptant style could encourage a client to be dependent on the counsellor and increase irrational beliefs about the need for others' love. Others might argue that although professional courtesy is a *sine qua non* of counselling practice, there is no particular onus on practitioners to feel or convey anything as grand or idealistic as UPR. Pragmatically, we might say that a high level of aspirational acceptance is necessary but this must be balanced by honesty, realism and therapeutic constraints.

Further reading

Bozarth, J. & Wilkins, P. (2001) *Rogers' Therapeutic Conditions: Evolution, Theory and Practice. Vol. 3. Unconscious Positive Regard.* Ross-on-Wye: PCCS.

2

How Important are Boundaries in Counselling Practice?

Boundaries or frames are taken to have considerable significance in therapeutic practice, so much so that transgressing some boundaries is tantamount to professional death, while others are open to interesting debate.

The clearest prohibitive boundary is that between the professional and the sexual relationship, discussed elsewhere in this book. Associated with this are boundaries between physical contact and non-contact, and between friendly relations and strictly professional relations. The standard classical psychoanalytic stance is that there should be no physical contact – no reassuring touch on the arm or shoulder, no hugs at times of great distress, and so on. (Some even avoid a simple handshake on first meeting.) There are good reasons for all this, including the avoidance of ambiguity and of unhelpful rescuing. Similarly, friendly and social relations between client and therapist are prohibited in the psychoanalytic tradition in order, again, to avoid ambiguity, and also to ensure the therapeutic relationship is purely focused on in-session transferential dynamics. In most humanistic approaches there may be some relaxing of such boundaries in the interests of authenticity and the judicious use of tactile contact for therapeutic purposes. Some cognitive and behavioural approaches may include a strategic use of out-of-office visits and in vivo therapeutic assignments, such as helping a client not to act out compulsions or to confront phobic objects. Clearly then, boundaries differ across models of therapy.

Boundaries may differ also according to individual therapist attitudes, decisions and risks. For example, what do you do if you see your client in public, or your client offers you a lift when it's raining? If your client has to go into hospital, has few friends and asks you to visit, will you agree? Some therapists maintain strict 'no compromise' policies for all such scenarios. Others may consider and agree on pragmatic, compassionate or therapeutic grounds. All should, however, carefully weigh up the benefits and costs: small acts can have large unintended consequences or meanings, and if you cross a boundary once, where might it lead?

Consider other boundary challenges. On timekeeping, it is thought very important by most psychoanalytic practitioners to offer consistent appointment times, to monitor clients' behaviour in relation to these and to make interpretations and hold to agreements. Rarely will they vary the session length deliberately or inadvertently. In certain humanistic approaches, however, sessions may be lengthened in order to facilitate and debrief after deep emotional therapeutic work, and behaviour therapy sometimes involves long intensive in vivo sessions. In addition, individual therapists may believe that flexibility is useful and simply human. Another well known boundary dictates that therapists should not accept gifts from clients since this introduces unconscious ambiguities associated with bribery and obligation: the therapeutic relationship should remain as purely professional as possible, even where it entails depths of emotion. Other boundaries include accepting only self-referrals and structuring the therapeutic environment so that clients never see each other. Again, different traditions, therapists and circumstances yield different responses to gifts and other scenarios.

So, apart from a universal agreement on the taboo against sexual contact, there are few absolute agreements on boundaries and the discussion seems mainly to reflect differences between traditions and their rationales. We might then ask whether any one approach has a better understanding of boundaries and, more generally, what the place of boundaries should be in counselling and psychotherapy. Undoubtedly some clients are mystified by boundaries that are unexplained, that are socially abnormal and that are perhaps hurtful or offensive. Heyward (1993) for example reported, as an ex-client of psychoanalytic psychotherapy, that she had actually felt abused by the rigid distance and coldness she experienced with her therapist. Boundaries, then, may be perceived as unhelpful rather than therapeutic, and we should wonder whether some traditional prohibitions may impact heavy-handedly on clients from different classes and cultures.

Professionalism presumably is important, both in the sense of observing necessary codes of ethical conduct and as a check against over-casual practices and subtle misunderstandings. In other words, boundaries have a real function. On the other hand, with the passing of time and an awareness of cultural changes and client perceptions, we might stop to consider the extent to which certain boundary traditions are or are not permanently important or adaptable. It is also possible to consider whether a strict adherence to boundaries may be crucial in relation to unconscious dynamics and simultaneously of little importance in the wider scheme of things. In other words, must we sometimes engage in an unavoidable paradox? Critical thinking on these matters shows that we cannot simply dispense with boundaries but neither can our traditions stand still.

Further reading

Heyward, C. (1993) *When Boundaries Betray Us: Beyond Illusions of What is Ethical in Therapy and Life*. San Francisco, CA: HarperCollins.

3

What Form Should Assessment Take?

The term 'assessment' means quite different things to different people, having connotations of school exams, clinical objectification and even unpleasant tax matters. There are often overlaps with and confusions about screening, diagnosis, case conceptualization and clinical hypothesizing. I want to use the term 'assessment' here in the following way. Anyone with an awareness of something not quite right in his or her life makes some assessment of whether it will get better or worse without attention, what it actually *is*, what its causes and remedies might be, whether others need to be involved and whether now is the time to consider seeing a counsellor. All mental health workers (including counsellors) must formulate some view of each new client, whether this involves an obligatory formal assessment or not. Even the most radically anti-assessment, practitioner would have to work hard not to entertain *some* impressions about a new client, based on experience and training. We all make assessments, whether minimalist or comprehensive, and the form of our assessments, depends on variables of training, profession, theoretical model and personal preferences.

At one extreme, some person-centred practitioners, opposed to any assessment that is perceived as imposed on the client by an expert, eschew assessment altogether: the client knows best and diagnostic assessment is an unnecessary and dangerous labelling exercise. At the other extreme, most psychiatrists and clinical psychologists are compelled to assess, often quite extensively and according to established psychodiagnostic categories, in the belief that treatment must fit rigorous diagnostic assessment. Somewhere in the middle of these extremes, many practitioners probably assess to one degree or another, as seems necessary to the client. For example, many clients using a bereavement counselling service have a 'simple' need to grieve and to feel understood. Yet others may have 'complex bereavement issues' including guilt, post-traumatic stress and other complicating social factors. Arnold Lazarus, the founder of multimodal therapy, acknowledges that in such cases clients probably do not need (or want) his 16-page assessment questionnaire, which at other times however can yield a richness of information to guide the therapeutic process.

Assessment helps to decide whether talking therapy is appropriate (the client may have stubborn psychiatric problems or undetected medical conditions) and whether what the service and counsellor offer matches the client's needs (for example, in terms of 'expertise', time available, etc.). Some psychoanalytic therapists assess for psychological-mindedness and a readiness to benefit from their form of therapy. This need not be done imperiously or 'behind the client's back' but can be done with full discussion and agreement. Indeed it is part of person-centred philosophy to be congruent about any concern that the counsellor has about her or his ability to be helpful.

Ongoing co-assessment is sometimes commended. In other words, any assessment of initial needs and aims can be done mutually. Another take on assessment is that we have far too little of it or far too little solid information to guide us. I find it surprising that so many counsellors take an anti-assessment stance, and seem much more interested in the client's history, in the depths of the therapeutic relationship and in insight and emotion. Assessment can be seen as looking at the client's terrain, as if co-creating a map of relevant details. It need not be an interrogative exercise couched in clinical terminology. I think it is responsible to clarify what the client needs and what she brings, as well as clarifying all possible areas of concern and helpfulness. Relevant areas can include the following:

- The presenting concern or concerns (and associated details).
- A pertinent personal and family history or narrative and current circumstances.
- Previous medical and psychological problems and any help received.
- The client's general preoccupations and fantasies, however apparently random.
- The client's own assessment of the causes of the current problem and related variables.
- The client's strengths, characteristics and general limitations.
- Related factors (religious, cultural, employment, financial, political, etc.).

These items help to create a picture of what is going on and possible causes. They need not all be applied but it is useful to keep them in mind. They help to generate hypotheses. They remind us that not everything is psychological (some emotional problems have medical causes). They should expand our understanding of the client. Potentially, they should also stimulate therapeutic thinking that goes beyond our approach-specific traditions of dysfunctional parenting, traumatic incidents and irrational thinking. They should help us to formulate tentative ways forward and also any indications for referral else-where. Of course further assessment items can be added and this can and should be done in a way that avoids a haphazard bombardment of questions. While some believe that therapist-initiated assessment is necessarily expertise-bolstering and undermines clients' existing strengths and self-healing, many do not believe this: assessment can be co-operative, iterative and 'light-touch'.

Further reading

Buckroyd, J. (2003) Using action research to develop an assessment system in a voluntary sector counselling service. *Counselling and Psychotherapy Research,* 3 (4): 278–284.

Feltham, C. (2006) Conceptualising clients' problems. In C. Feltham and I. Horton (eds), *The Sage Handbook of Counselling and Psychotherapy* (2nd edn). London: Sage.

Is Eclecticism as Bad as the Bad Press it's Had?

Since eclecticism has been referred to as an undisciplined, haphazard 'mish-mash' and the BACP adopted its principle of core theoretical models for accredited courses and individuals, eclecticism has been eclipsed by integrationism. Eclecticism has been portrayed as the haphazard process of throwing around techniques with no coherent rationale and with likely poor results for clients. By contrast, integrative models are portrayed as coherent theoretical blends of other models, preferably no more than two models elegantly brought together in, say, a new, probably hyphenated model. Eclecticism is unskilful, resting on inadequate training and hit-or-miss practice, runs the argument, while integrationism is a skilful, defensible endeavour. A major consequence of this perception or belief is that models and practitioners referred to as integrative have flourished (a majority of practitioners now identify as integrative) while eclecticism and eclectic counsellors seem to have gone underground or extinct, or expediently refer to their work as integrative.

What's in a name? According to some, 'integrative' is simply a more elegant and acceptable name for eclecticism. During many discussions on this topic, I have found that a lot of students and supervisees feel strongly that they need and want to respond to each of their clients in a unique and tailored manner. Most feel strongly that the imposition of a 'pure' model would ignore important individual differences between clients. In this analysis of matters, it is the inflexibly delivered pure model that constitutes poor practice, while eclecticism is an attempt to choose those techniques (and relationship styles) that best fit client needs. Some of these same students concede that it could be the case that a hard won integrative approach – for example, by spending many years training in two or more models – might ultimately help clients better.

This view seems to be based on the anxiety that techniques utilized without a thorough familiarity with their underlying theories might not be quite as skilful as otherwise. However, there seems to be no evidence that this is true. And there is an obvious case against this approach, which is its cost and elitism: very lengthy training must usually be paid for by practitioners themselves (therefore only those affluent enough to do so could pursue this path) and eventually these costs might well be passed on to clients.

Another argument against lengthy training for integrative practice is its randomness. In other words, almost any two (or more) approaches might be trained in, regardless of their effectiveness or the likelihood that they would work well together. Such integrationism might appear thorough and beyond reproach but would seem to place such integrationism in a similar position to eclecticism (in its maligned form); that is, you may choose any combination you like, willy-nilly. We would here be elevating appearance over reality when our main concern should always be what clients actually need. In principle our best guidance for this should be evidence gleaned from rigorous research, but there is still relatively little in the way of randomized control trials comparing a significant number of therapies.

Back to eclecticism itself. It is not necessarily the case that eclectic practice is haphazard. 'Theoretically consistent eclecticism' rests on the choice of techniques from any approach that can be rationalized as fitting into the blueprint of the practitioner's principal model. Gerard Egan has at times referred to his 'skilled helper' approach as systematic eclecticism. Arnold Lazarus calls his multimodal therapy 'technical eclecticism' in order to emphasize his belief that it is techniques (what therapists do) rather than theories that effect therapeutic change. Lazarus furthermore uses a framework (the BASIC ID) for deciding on technique selection. Just to add to this catalogue of perspectives on eclecticism, Sol Garfield entitled a major textbook *Psychotherapy: An Eclectic-Integrative Approach*. This both reflects the wisdom of taking the best from many approaches and integrating them but also reflects the fact that some cultures are simply not as negatively excited as the British about eclecticism. It is probably inconceivable in the UK counselling scene that such a hyphenated term could even be used.

It is quite possible that some practitioners are inadequately trained and that when they use techniques wildly, in an ill-judged manner – particularly potentially damaging techniques (such as regressive interventions) – they represent a threat to clients and subsequently to the profession. But isn't it equally possible that some who have trained very thoroughly in one approach, or indeed in two approaches, may inappropriately attempt to fit clients with those models? Much more thought and honesty is needed about the pros and cons involved here.

Further reading

Garfield, S. (1995) *Psychotherapy: An Eclectic-Integrative Approach* (2nd edn).
New York: Wiley.

What are the Pros and Cons of Short-term, Time-limited Counselling?

In the 1980s very few in the UK talked about time-limited counselling. This was because for decades most counselling and psychotherapy, and certainly all psychoanalysis, was presumed to be open-ended. That is, it took as long as it took, and this usually meant at least many months and often many years. A combination of factors forced the time-limited agenda onto the counselling community. The development of certain humanistic and cognitive behavioural therapies challenged the dominance of psychoanalytic practice from around the 1960s and 1970s. The emergence of managed care and employee assistance programmes (EAPs) in the USA obliged therapists to consider how long their work took. Research began to emerge showing that a majority of clients often wanted, and benefited from, around six sessions rather than much longer. Many sought 'symptom relief' in the shortest possible time rather than extensive exploration of putative, multiple, subtle psychological factors. Students using free university counselling services, for example, tended to take up on average only four or five sessions (Feltham, 1997). The growth of counselling in the NHS (and also in EAPs and elsewhere) gradually forced the question of funding in relation to resources and effectiveness, and the problem of waiting lists had to be faced. It was in the interests of private practitioners not to think about short-term therapy, which self-evidently means higher throughput of clients and therefore harder work as well as, perhaps, less job satisfaction.

It is much more obvious what the advantages of time-limited therapy are to clients than to practitioners. Let's put aside those relatively affluent clients who seek long-term therapy in order to reflect in a leisurely and perhaps aspirational manner on their lives. Most people feel impelled to seek help in a crisis or when things have gone wrong yet again. While psychoanalysts and psycho-analytic therapists themselves internalize a model of long-term, purportedly in-depth self-examination in their own mandatory and costly training therapy, most clients (or so I argue here) wish for a reasonably rapid reduction in bad feelings, distressing thoughts and unhelpful behaviours. While psychoanalytic practitioners warn against 'flight into health' and 'symptom substitution', an increasing majority of clients and counsellors in the NHS and other funded settings want to ease suffering promptly and provide emotional support and constructive insights. Presumably, person-centred practitioners respect every client's self-determined pace and are ready to end whenever the client is ready. It so happens that the psychoanalytic practitioner profits financially from lengthy therapy as well as believing in its necessity, and the person-centred practitioner may benefit financially if in private practice but believes very strongly in following the therapeutic process and refraining from the intro-duction and use of any technical shortcuts.

Now consider the funder, whether the NHS or other organization. Even if these were persuaded that long-term therapy was necessary and beneficial in most cases, funding could not be made available for unknown quantities of long-term therapy. And while a relatively small number of clients might get added benefits from lengthier therapy, many would languish on waiting lists. I am not addressing here the equation involving a saner world society in which, say, the abolition of expensive weaponry could perhaps offset the cost of better healthcare. If we took that route we would still need to weigh up the merits of cancer treatment and hip replacements, say, against more and longer psychological therapies. Some counsellors in their well-intentioned, perhaps romantic and utopian way, do sometimes imagine that infinite resources are available. It might be nice for everyone who wants it to have as much therapy as she or he desires, and it would be nice to resource a much greater number of counsellors and therapists. But this isn't going to happen.

Some of the disadvantages of time-limited therapy are already implicit in the above discussion. Sometimes the removal of one symptom does lead to the emergence of another; indeed it may sometimes take months before someone can establish sufficient trust and contact or disclose repressed traumatic memories. It may sometimes be wasteful – a false economy – to fund short-term interventions when the likelihood of relapse can be predicted. We can certainly observe the machinations of the promoters of Increasing Access to Psychological Therapies (IAPT) with its 'stepped care' aims, alongside the call-centre style of CBT delivery, compared with much more intense, careful, face to face and long-term therapies. Years from now we may be ruing the investment in such false economy, quick-fix shortcuts and their (predicted by some) high failure rates over time.

The best compromise is perhaps to offer and evaluate therapy of varied lengths and time spans and in general to reconsider the temporal factor altogether – one-offs, short-term, longer sessions, intermittent therapy across the lifespan, very long-term and so on. Where some practitioners are vehemently opposed to time constraints, let them at least demonstrate a thought-out argument on the matter.

Further reading

Feltham, C. (1997) *Time-Limited Counselling*. London: Sage.

6

What's Wrong with Counsellor Self-disclosure?

Most approaches to counselling recommend that counsellor self-disclosure is either absent or minimal. A counsellor who shares too much personal information is likely to take attention away from the client, perhaps even encourage the client to 'counsel' or feel sorry for or protective towards the counsellor. (This is to overlook those few humanistic and existentialist therapists who have espoused as much openness as possible.) Too much counsellor self-disclosure is taken by most practitioners as a sign that the counsellor has unresolved personal problems. However, purposeful, skilful and timely 'countertransference disclosure' or congruent disclosures on the part of the counsellor are thought to be sometimes helpful. For some clients, hearing that the practitioner has experienced sexual abuse, a drink problem or bereavement, for example, and has lived through and perhaps overcome its distressing effects, can be reassuring. A relative minority of therapists eschew such reassurance altogether, wanting clients to be able to be wholly themselves with all their fears and fantasies. And some regard the counsellor as being in a parental role, or at least in a position of perceived strength so that the client can feel safe and if necessary regress. But an absolute refusal to disclose anything about oneself is sometimes thought too rigid and dehumanizing. So counsellors tread a fine line.

In general most of us like to be listened to. Attentive and asymmetrical listening is unusual in our society. But there are some little-considered aspects of counsellor 'abstinence' that it may be useful to examine here. The attentive, unconditional acceptance offered by a counsellor can give a client the impression that everything he or she has to say is fascinating. Perhaps that is the case in the view of some counsellors, but I have heard enough supervisees expressing their exasperation at client small-talk to doubt it. Granted that some clients find such unusual attention initially disquieting, most come to value it. Rarely is it a counsellor's intention that a client should relate everything that comes to mind, no matter how trivial (the psychoanalyst may appear to encourage this but does so for interpretative purposes). Counsellors tend to disdain too much small talk or chit-chat, often regarding it as defensive. Indeed most counselling skills subtly shape clients' talk in the direction of problem identification, emotionally meaningful material and goal-setting. But the asocial, asymmetrical nature of counselling, much of it based on an unnatural withholding of the counsellor's talk about self, creates something of a void that a client comes to fill. Aristotle suggested that nature abhors a vacuum and it is often noted that human beings tend to be restless pattern-seekers, perhaps especially in situations with a deprivation of normal stimuli.

Another interesting aspect of counsellor abstinence from self-disclosure (and from expressing personal opinions) is that the client's fantasies (or phantasies) about the counsellor are thereby fuelled. Anyone with a mysterious vocation like a counsellor, with a corresponding job title and perhaps an associated private setting to match, is likely to come across as having expertise, even if this is inwardly eschewed by many counsellors. If you come in distress and confusion to a job-titled counsellor or psychotherapist, you are almost sure to imagine that she or he has some mastery of life that you do not have. You would not knowingly go to see a counsellor who had significant unresolved distress and confusion of their own. But, in spite of counsellors' and psychotherapists' training, including personal therapy, personal development work and ongoing supervision, we have no effective way of knowing whether any practitioner at any one time carries distress and confusion. Practitioners themselves may be unaware of it, or aware of it but inclined to deny or conceal it. And in my view it is almost certainly true that none of us is immune from the everyday ravages of the human condition. In any case, usually the person in the client role (talking about herself, paying the money, and so on) is in the spotlight, vulnerable. Most of us would probably not pour our hearts out to a stranger if we believed that they were as distressed or confused as we were (or perhaps even more distressed). Most of us are sensitized to a right to privacy and personal discretion for all citizens, and this certainly includes therapists – but many therapists deliberately practise a paradoxical withholding of self, alongside an expectation that the client will freely disclose.

Let's consider if this ever were indeed the case, if it necessarily matters. It's possible that just at the time you (the client) started seeing a counsellor (Karen) she had recently begun going through a divorce. In principle (according to professional, ethical guidelines), if this were sufficiently distressing to her, she would temporarily cease practising; but this is unrealistic if Karen depends, as most of us do, on her everyday work for economic survival. She may well try to offload some of her distress on to a supervisor or therapist but this would be no guarantee that she won't still be distressed. Now, the asymmetrical nature of counselling (the client discloses, the counsellor doesn't) means that the client is very unlikely to know about Karen's divorce and its upsetting effects. In general the practice of counsellor non-self-disclosure unintentionally feeds the fantasy that counsellors don't have personal problems – because, after all, their selection and rigorous training would have minimized these.

We sometimes forget too that we cannot *not* disclose certain things about ourselves – by the way we speak and dress, our appearance and demeanour in general, even by where we live and at what level of comfort, if we are in private practice. The real choice may be, then, between minimal non-verbal self-disclosure, occasional therapeutically purposeful disclosures, and at the other (rare) extreme, a willingness to be highly transparent.

Further reading

Farber, B.A. (2006) *Self-Disclosure in Psychotherapy.* New York: Guilford.
Jourard, S. (1964) *The Transparent Self.* Princeton, NJ: Van Nostrand.

How Crucial are Counselling Ethics?

It is sometimes said that 'ethics is the cornerstone of counselling' and this seems such a weighty and indisputable statement that few would contest or question it. There does, of course, have to be some sort of agreed safety net and set of norms for something that aspires to become a profession. The BACP *Ethical Framework for Good Practice in Counselling and Psychotherapy* replaced former codes of ethics and practice that had come to be regarded as too complicated and prescriptive. Hence, this framework sets out the basic guiding principles. These begin with core values which include respect and fairness; they mention desirable personal qualities such as empathy, sincerity and wisdom; and they spell out applications in practice, teaching, supervision and research. They are also linked with complaints procedures. The *Framework* is a key document in addressing problems and complaints. Key areas within it concern confidentiality, personal and sexual contact and compromised effectiveness. Something that most courses are not equipped to do is to present and debate the origins of the moral philosophy underpinning professional ethics, as well as examining individuals' areas of uncertainty, weakness and temptation.

Unable to agree on counselling theory though many counsellors are (recall the 400+ models), all seem agreed on confidentiality and the taboo on sexual contact. It's hard to find anything to say against confidentiality, except that it is stretched by the exemptions for supervision and possible harm to self and others. No-one can guarantee absolute confidentiality when there may be several members of a supervision group, for example, and when supervisors themselves are required sometimes to discuss their work with others, in an indeterminate chain. Confidentiality in practice has to be taken on trust while any detected and serious breach of it should be met with appropriate measures. What we do not seem to have developed is a systematic means of making links between transgressions and the psychological causes of these in individuals so that we can learn to avoid such harm. We might, however, agree that it is probably fantasy to imagine that we could ever wholly eradicate ethical transgressions.

While almost every practitioner agrees on the taboo against sexual contact – since it violates trust, abuses power and changes the nature of the relationship – not all would agree on the limits involved. For example, some insist on an absolute, lifelong ban, while others suggest the ban can be lifted at the termination of therapy or after some agreed period, say a few months. This is complicated since some therapeutic relationships are lengthy and intense while others are brief and not intense. There is also the objection that it is against our human rights to dictate who can or cannot have sex with whom. In some other professions this is also a grey area. Greyer still, perhaps, are questions about flirting, kissing, innuendo and sexual suggestiveness. Therapists are not shy about admitting that erotic transferential and countertransferential dynamics are potentially ever-present. But again, there are different views on these matters; most agree transgressions should not happen but some would want to distinguish between degrees of transgression and effects on the client involved. It is often assumed that the perpetrators are mainly the practitioners and also mainly men but this is not necessarily the case. Clients and women (whether clients or practitioners) are also quite capable of making sexual advances and counsellors – however principled – are capable of making mistakes. Obviously by its nature this is an area that is very difficult to research. Sexual contact in counselling is regarded as the 'big taboo', second to other kinds of dual relationship, but these overlook the question of forgiveness (should a practitioner lose his or her livelihood over a forgivable mistake?) and other, possibly more common and neglected areas of ethics.

Counsellors are required to monitor their effectiveness and not to exploit their clients. There is arguably less chance of ineffectiveness and exploitation incurring financial and health costs in short-term and 'free' therapy than in private practice. Counsellors in the NHS do not take money from clients, do not generally see them for very long, and are connected with other health professionals and familiar with NICE guidelines. Counsellors in private practice tend to see clients for longer (in some cases for years), they do take money directly and they may or may not have close links with health professionals and a familiarity with NICE guidelines. Indeed as far as I am aware they are not obliged to be so aware and may have philosophical and clinical objections to such criteria. Some counsellors and psychotherapists do not regard their work as a health profession at all.

This combination of circumstances leads to the situation where private practitioners (particularly in psychoanalytic and humanistic approaches) are arguably the ones most likely to be complained against. Whatever their 'ethics', their practice can be compromised by the above factors, and there is a possible temptation to skimp on continuing professional development due to its costs. I have little idea how common the situation is wherein a private practitioner sees a client for many years with little to show in the way of an effective outcome. But publications by dissatisfied clients have tended to attribute blame to practitioners in private psychoanalytic practice more than to others.

Given the headlight attention that abuses of confidentiality and sexual contact have had, it seems strange that relatively little attention is given to, and complaints made about, counsellor ineffectiveness. Serious delays can be implicated in a client not getting the right help, as well as a serious loss of money. Compared with these, problems of sexual contact and confidentiality may be seen as not necessarily the worst abuses or instances of disservice. Professional ethics in counselling are obviously important but we should not overlook the possibility that, for all their positive public relations reassurance impact, ethical statements generally fail to give due importance to effectiveness. The reason for this, I suspect, is that we cannot agree on best methods among the 400 or so approaches and their internal techniques; we do not have an agreement about psychodiagnostic validity; we can always 'blame the client' for not complying or for being resistant (and some clients may fit these descriptions); and indeed we have no consensus as to whether counselling and psychotherapy are health-oriented professions or even professions at all.

Behind ethical statements about 'best practice' is the overlooked domain of definitions and aims. Ethics are crucial but they are lame if a significant number of clients are not getting effective help. Since much research suggests that counselling is 80 per cent effective (and even this can be disputed), it is still possible that one in five clients receives unsatisfactory therapeutic attention. It would not be ethical to dispense with or play down our ethics but it is possible that for our own convenience we will unethically and tacitly avoid at the highest levels contentious areas like effectiveness.

It can also be said that ethics underpin everything that therapy, and everything in this book, are about. When any of us becomes aware of levels of psychological suffering and thinks that we might like to try to do something about it, our choice is an ethical one. I could give money to a mental health charity. I could, like the Buddha, give profound attention to the movement of suffering inside myself. I could decide that suffering arises or worsens in unequal, 'selfish capitalist' societies and do something actively political about this. The choice to become a psychotherapist or counsellor is an ethical decision about resources and perceived causes and remedies, as well as being about personal preferences. The choice to research the micro-ethics of, say, minor ethical infringements rather than to research more substantive topics is an ethical choice. This isn't to say that we must choose between ethics and therapeutics, but to call for an awareness of proportions. Of course there are abusive professionals in all walks of life, and any of us could in a moment of weakness or misjudgement fall foul of ethical standards. But there are also systemic weaknesses and misjudgements in our professional bodies and training courses that cause unhappiness and stress (because fallible human beings drive systems). For some reason we do not refer to these as unethical.

Further reading

Bond, T. (2009) *Standards and Ethics for Counselling in Action* (3rd edn). London: Sage.
Bates, Y. & House, R. (eds) (2003) *Ethically Challenged Professions*. Ross-on-Wye: PCCS.
Gabriel, L. (2005) *Speaking the Unspeakable: The Ethics of Dual Relationships in Counselling and Psychotherapy*. London: Routledge.

8

Can You Counsel Effectively When Affected by Illness or Personal Troubles?

It is recognized by professional bodies that practitioners should monitor their own physical and mental health, that problems should be discussed in supervision, and that in certain circumstances they should consider withdrawing from practice until they are healthier and more fully available for clients. It is also very common for counsellors and psychotherapists to engage in their own therapy before or during their practice, and part of the rationale for this is preventative. However, it is not clear whether these principles can always be realistically operationalized.

Take some examples of the kinds of events that might significantly compromise the mental or emotional health of counsellors: separation and divorce; bereavement; post-traumatic stress; work stress (e.g. high caseloads); accidents and illnesses; being a crime victim; financial problems; family conflicts and problems; caring responsibilities; the effects of ageing. In addition, anyone can experience transient depression and anxiety. In principle, employed counsellors can take any necessary sick leave, and the self-employed should have sickness insurance. But in practice employers are not always understanding, too much sick leave may not be practicable, and sickness insurance is expensive.

Most of us will experience times of relatively brief injury or infection, for example, and have to (and can) bear a week or two off work without too much disruption. But protracted or frequent periods of illness – including post-viral fatigue – are another matter because client appointments have to be cancelled, waiting lists may build, colleagues may have to take on the extra work, and the uncertainty for and vulnerability of some clients will have to be considered. The practical and clinical impact of longer absences is, then, one major consideration. I have not considered here the 'equal opportunities' implications for those with disabilities or limitations that either periodically or continuously impact on their ability to work consistently.

When it comes to personal troubles that are not primarily about physical illness, there are complications. For the most part people are not given extensive paid leave to address the problems of divorce, which can drag on for many months or even years, creating emotional and financial problems along the way. If you experience a combination of problems such as divorce, illness and ageing (say, in your fifties or sixties), yet need to hang on to your counselling practice as your sole source of income, what should be your ethical action?

I have sometimes heard the claim, and indeed have experienced this myself, that in periods of crisis one may actually find 'refuge' in counselling practice, in the discipline of listening intently to another and suspending one's own preoccupations. Some have even commented that personal turmoil can helpfully re-immerse you in the raw pain that many clients are feeling, while a practitioner whose life is 'too good' may become unintentionally distant from clients' suffering. The publicized personal breakdowns of Jung and some other therapists attest to the value of such experiences for wounded healers.

My contention is that the professional ethics of counselling, while completely well-meaning, create a fantasy that all practitioners are or should be extremely mentally fit, relatively untroubled and able to deal effectively with any difficulties that do occur. This fantasy is likely to discourage practitioners from being open about their problems. Idealistic ethics are also likely to make some practitioners hide their troubles.

There is probably also a hidden class dimension. If you are the sole breadwinner in your family and also on a very modest and tight income, you could not afford to withdraw nobly from your work for a period while you sort things out. On the other hand, if you have a fairly privileged lifestyle and an affluent partner, you may well be able to take time out or at least to reduce your workload. I don't think anyone would explicitly argue that counselling should be practised only by the affluent but the call for a temporary withdrawal from work implicitly overlooks the real situation of the majority on modest or low incomes. This is a point that professional body policy makers need to consider carefully – exactly how are practitioners who are temporarily compromised to address such matters *realistically*?

Perhaps there is a thorny conceptual issue here too: I have spoken above of people *suffering* and this term is used relatively rarely, and indeed disliked, by some counselling writers who prefer to emphasize personal strength and agency. Suffering may connote helpless victimhood. I do not develop this topic much here but it is pertinent to ask whether we do not all suffer, and sometimes suffer for prolonged periods. This view is at odds with being portrayed as heroically addressing and resolving all our problems promptly. Should therapists be such prompt and effective all-round problem-solvers in their own lives that few psychosomatic, emotional or financial problems ever occur for them?

Further reading

Dryden, W. (1992) *The Dryden Interviews* (Chapter 9: The counsellor and ME: An interview with Pat Milner). London: Whurr.

Orlans, V. (1993) The counsellor's life crisis. In W. Dryden (ed.), *Questions and Answers on Counselling in Action*. London: Sage.

9

Does it Matter if Empathy is not Matched by Personal Experience?

The personal experience I refer to here is the counsellor's, and I have in mind those times when clients bring experiences and stories that the counsellor may have no experience of herself. For example, the client may be bereaved, divorcing, elderly, bisexual, disabled, anxiously facing an imminent promotion or redundancy, or battling addiction. If the counsellor has no such similar experience, she can still of course closely track the client's feelings and meanings, experience some degree of accurate understanding and convey this to the client. Indeed this is one of the most key skills of any counsellor. Now, it's clear that none of us as counsellors can have experienced the full range of possible traits and states, events, dilemmas and struggles that we may meet in clients. Perhaps it's ridiculous to imagine we could ever come close.

But to what extent can a man know what menstruation, pregnancy, miscarriage, birth and menopause feel like, for example? How accurately and emotionally can a heterosexual man understand a gay man's sexuality and experiences of homophobia? In many addiction counselling agencies it has been traditional to employ staff who are themselves 'in recovery' and therefore able fully to understand their clients' experiences. Many years ago I counselled a woman in her sixties who, recently retired and single, was agonizing over whether to move house to another part of the country to be near relatives. At the time I thought I had understood her well but years later, as I faced similar issues for the first time, the anxiety, loneliness and practical difficulties involved hit me much more personally and made me wonder in retrospect if she had sensed the limitations of my understanding.

Of course, the capacity for emotional and imaginative empathy probably varies considerably from person to person and from time to time. Many counsellors report being viscerally affected by clients' stories during sessions. Many find it helpful to read up on subjects outside their own experience, including relevant fiction. We probably all know that it's possible to call on our most similar emotional experiences in order to understand another's. For example, you may never have experienced an acute bereavement but memory of the impact of once losing your job, house or marriage may go some way towards appreciating another's experience of the loss of a partner by death.

The really important question here is what effect our limitations have on clients. When we engage in disciplined empathy, might it come across to some clients as *pretending* to understand? If so, it might well undermine the congruence of the relationship. If the client feels unconvinced by the counsellor's demeanour, he or she may drop out of counselling: 'How can she help me? She's too privileged to understand my poverty/too young to appreciate the struggles of old age'. Counsellors will of course often congruently convey such mismatches or lacunae: for example, 'I can't pretend to understand how hard that must be for you'. But even such a deployment of interpersonal skills won't always convince clients that they're really being heard or that effective help will be found.

Another dimension to this matter is that you may have had a similar experience but many years ago. For example, you may have been very poor and struggled to make ends meet in your youth but have since done well by one means and another. Although you can dimly remember your own experiences of poverty, they are now faint, they may be a little painful for you to recall and you may even have some sense that, if you transcended your own poverty, your client should be able to do likewise. It does happen sometimes that we put the past behind us in this way and may even change our personal and political views across the decades. An older person with varied life experiences will not necessarily be able to use these in helping another. The client might well, in any case, feel inadequate at discussing her financial struggles if she is being counselled in private practice in your affluent home, the non-verbal, visual message being that she should be able to pull herself out of poverty just as the counsellor presumably has done. Conversely the younger counsellor might struggle to fully understand and convey her understanding of her much older client's disillusionment with wealth if she herself is in the early stages of aspiring to material wealth.

Ideally, we can clear our minds of our own memories, values and wishes within sessions in order to fully attend to the client and empathize with his or her particular issues. In a sense counselling demands both this kind of emptiness or receptivity at the same time as fellow-feeling (often drawn from a similar experience) is needed. All these factors matter – none of us can be the perfect counsellor, but neither should we be weighed down by awareness of the gaps between our own and our clients' experiences. On the other hand, the question of client–counsellor matching won't simply go away: are clients helped better by therapists with similar life experiences?

Further reading

Freire, E.S. (2007) Empathy. In M. Cooper, M. O'Hara, P.F. Schmid & G. Wyatt (eds), *The Handbook of Person-Centred Psychotherapy and Counselling*. Houndmills: Palgrave.

Rowan, J. & Jacobs, M. (2002) *The Therapist's Use of Self*. Maidenhead: Open University Press.

Everyday Counselling Practice:

Challenge

Provide a robust defence for conventional views on the topics in this group. In other words, argue with the author's views where these go against the prevailing norms or your own views. Weigh up what is called 'good practice' or 'received wisdom' against the right to a responsible challenge. Consider what the author says in the light of your experience and developing practice, and find ways to articulate any disagreement. You might also identify any areas where the author isn't critical enough for your liking.

Case Study

Martin is a mature and confident person with a naturally enquiring disposition. His practice seems to thrive and clients respond well to his authentic, compassionate and flexible style. Feeling that accreditation is probably necessary to progress his career, he reluctantly goes through the application process. Although a very skilled writer, he baulks at the requirement to name his approach and to make it look more coherent than he believes any counselling really is. In practice, he doesn't always observe time boundaries, he freely self-discloses (his life is sometimes chaotic) and he admits to working eclectically. He applies for accreditation but his application is not accepted. Should he modify his practice? Should he re-apply and disingenuously modify the way he describes his practice? Might it be said that his professional body fails to appreciate the effectiveness of his actual counselling and to extend unconditional positive professional regard to him? (See Lomas, 1993.)

Critical thinking perspectives

Martin might find that he cannot compromise his own values, in which case he could (a) continue in practice but remain unaccredited; (b) reapply with some small changes but also give a full statement of his values and reasons for differing from the evaluators, and then accept the consequences; (c) terminate his membership and join another organization such as the Independent Practitioners Network; (d) publicize his own views and create his own network or organization. These options all, however, contain some risks and further compromises, and require further energy: Martin is only human and he might succumb to depression, in which case we could infer that professional requirements as stressors can sometimes be responsible for causing or exacerbating mental health problems. Many sociological and philosophical issues can be found here.

Training and Curriculum Issues

Is Training Necessary?

This is the kind of question that is greeted either with an incredulous splutter ('Of *course* it's necessary!') or the suspicion that the author is (or *I am*) being deliberately provocative, perhaps in a juvenile manner. It is also a question that is sometimes put by naïve or critical outsiders who do not believe that counselling requires any special skill. But there are some good reasons besides these for asking it.

Few would dispute the necessity to provide rigorous medical training, since medicine is a life and death matter with associated high risks of negligence, malpractice and terrible consequences. But at the other end of the training scale we are entitled to ask whether training is always necessary or possible in the fields of, say, art, drama, teaching, politics. One can be an amateur artist or actor (or even an untrained professional one) without doing harm, and some professionals in those fields have been candid enough to admit that 'there's nothing to it'. It's possible to have natural talent and/or to train oneself in some areas. Some would argue seriously that art *cannot* be taught (Elkins, 2001). Teaching once used to be a profession requiring no specific training. Members of the British parliament require no specific qualifications in politics in order to do their very responsible jobs. Indeed parents are not required to undergo any training for what is sometimes called the most important job in the world.

People were engaged in listening to others' personal problems long before counselling or psychotherapy trainings were devised. Clearly, the founders of most therapeutic approaches could not have been trained in those methods since they themselves created their own models of counselling. Freud never had a Freudian training, nor Jung a Jungian one. We are now in a position where no-one can credibly become a counsellor without a minimum of two or three years of training. On the face of it this makes sense. Addressing others' personal, emotional problems is a responsible business and where money, health and professional identity are concerned a seal of approval on training standards and content is probably essential. But let's look at some of the problems in the counselling training field:

1   Any agreement on how long a training should be seems based on arbitrary notions – over 400 hours according to BACP course accreditation criteria, but why? Who arrives at such figures and how? A minimum of two to three years is the rule of thumb for counselling training, but a minimum of three to four years is the case for psychotherapy training. Why? Superficially, the answer is about a coverage of topics, placements and personal development. A great deal of psychoanalytic training is about the trainee's own analysis, something which is missing from some counselling training; on the other hand, intensive skills training may be missing from psychoanalytic training.

2   There is no consensus on curriculum content. The BACP now require coverage of the relevant ethics, law, mental health, psychopharmacology, research, core theoretical model (CTM) skills and theory, and self-awareness and supervised practice, and it is generally expected that courses will contain some material on professional issues, developmental/lifespan issues and theories of approaches apart from the core model (comparative models). But – as is spelled out elsewhere in this book – courses being based on a wide variety of CTMs means that content will vary enormously from course to course. One that disputes the very notion of psychodiagnostic assessment presumably possesses little on this, while courses based on existentialist principles will have relatively little on micro-skills or techniques, and others may be technique-heavy and theory-light.

3   Generally it has been accepted that counselling training should be face to face and that online training would be insufficient. But the growth of online facilities and capacity potentially means that lectures and demonstration videos can be placed online, essays can be submitted online and group conferencing is feasible online, and one can envisage the submission of actual counselling practice online with tutor feedback also online. It may not be optimal but it's possible to envisage at least some training happening in this way, thus making training more flexible and reducing the need for lengthy attendances and associated costs.

4   A good deal of training material, especially theory, is derived from published texts, and there is no reason to think that students cannot learn a large proportion of what they need from books and other texts, much of this also accessible online. Reinforced by other multimedia materials, this can be an effective way of learning about counselling. If necessary, exams can be used to test knowledge. It is also surprising that vivas are so seldom used when counselling practice depends so much on interpersonal skills.

5   Returning to the problem of how much training is necessary, we make the assumption that all students need the same amount. Consider the little-researched probability that some trainees are more intelligent, personable, talented and suitable than others, and we might entertain the idea that each requires a personalized, differently tailored training. Some may need a longer training than others, indeed some might gain most of what they need from online sources and private reading. The Scottish psychoanalyst Ronald Fairbairn, for example, was largely self-trained.

6   One argument for live group attendance over a period of time is that people learn much of what is necessary from their interaction with others, in personal development groups, counselling skills practice and simply the cut and thrust of interaction, of relating, giving and receiving feedback and dealing with a variety of other people and interpersonal challenges. This seems so but could perhaps be achieved by more direct and more efficient means, for example by more time being spent in personal development groups.

7   Linked with 5 (above) is the observation that some trainees appear to gain a lot from their training while others do not, and yet most still receive their qualification and stand an equal chance of getting a job as a counsellor (if they are lucky). There is no way of measuring finely (or even quite crudely) individual counsellors' competencies, yet it is fairly likely that some are better than others with the same qualification. Training itself therefore is not so much a seal of approval of competencies as a statement that someone has attended a course and passed all the required elements, many of them academic.

8   There is as yet no agreement on whether counselling training must be academically situated or overseen, nor on whether the academic element necessarily ensures better training. And in addition we have not agreed on what academic level of training is necessary in order to license those who are trained to work with (which) client groups with (what) presenting concerns.

9   It has often been noted by sociologists of the professions that selection, recruitment, training and qualifications, endorsed by further and higher education and professional bodies, form part of a process designed to persuade the public that these are respectable people with specialized skills who deserve professional status. Critics of many of the professions would argue that these are no more than rituals required by a capitalist, bureaucratic society and that they are always somewhat illusory.

10 Finally, it is a sobering thought that at least some research comparing trained with untrained counsellors has found little difference in client outcomes (McLellan, 1999).

We may agree that some sort of training is necessary but the parameters seem highly arbitrary and subject to the politics and whims of professional bodies. What we can seem to be sure of is that training always becomes in time more lengthy, more demanding, pitched at a higher academic level, and more costly – thus usually if not always becoming the preserve of the more affluent middle classes.

Further reading

McLellan, J. (1999) Becoming an effective psychotherapist or counsellor: are training and supervision necessary? In C. Feltham (ed.), *Controversies in Psychotherapy and Counselling.* London: Sage.

Who is Suitable to be a Counsellor?

Selection processes at interviews for counselling courses are taken seriously. There is fairly widespread agreement that applicants for counselling training need to show certain qualities. Acceptance, warmth, genuineness, insightful-ness, non-defensiveness, integrity, maturity, intelligence and an absence of arrogance, prejudice, rigidity – these are presumably obvious and non-contentious desirable qualities for a potential counsellor. Resilience is prob-ably necessary, and particularly a good level of current robustness, that is, not being in crisis or highly vulnerable. It can be very difficult to determine these qualities via brief interviews, and group interviews can sometimes bring these more to the fore.

I am fairly sure, from years of experience of co-interviewing, that a complete consensus on who is suitable is non-existent. Often there is agreement but sometimes there is sharp disagreement. The candidate appears calm, thoughtful and full of potential to one interviewer but nervous, dull and average to the other. (Since counsellors as interviewers are likely to be non-judgemental they may not use such terminology but that doesn't mean they do not subjectively, privately, sometimes think such thoughts.) There may also be some tacit pressure on interviewers to recruit on the basis of a mixed range of students in any intake.

Since very few grants exist for counselling training, talented but penniless people may not be able to readily secure training for themselves. In other words, as well as having suitable personal qualities he or she must have enough money to pay their way through training. We might argue that those suitable as counsellors should be heroically determined to be resourceful and withstand hardships like struggling to find money for the training. In this category too are those – often women – who cannot find ways around childcare commitments, or those who are very promising and begin training but have to drop out due to these commitments or intervening life events.

I shall raise the question elsewhere about the personal qualities of the counsellor possibly being more important than theory and technique. Successful counselling may depend more on the person of the counsellor, and her creativity, intelligence and presence, than on how well she imbibes the ingredients of training and passes course assignments. Related to this, but generally considered too embarrassing to discuss, is the possibility that some counsellors are somewhat unimaginative and uncreative, some are mediocre, and yet others – perhaps a minority – are outstanding. We cannot, however, identify and pluck out from the general populace those who possess the potential to be excellent therapists since we can only choose between those who put themselves forward to become counsellors. Employers can usually only choose between those who complete training courses and become accredited. Clients can only choose a private practitioner from among those who set themselves up in that capacity. There isn't necessarily a correlation between the most suitable (and excellent) and those who finally become available to clients.

Should counsellors have a great deal of 'life experience'? That is, does struggling through various obstacles, losses and traumas and learning from these necessarily make you a better counsellor? This is the wounded healer hypothesis which, in spite of an intuitive appeal to many, has little evidence to support it. But it does seem that someone who has led a charmed life of great privilege and little adversity may struggle to understand others' misfortunes. We must recognize, however, that no-one can have experienced all or even most of the problems encountered by a range of clients. Nor can any counsellor be simultaneously male and female, black and white, or possess other impossible combinations of qualities that might give them wide-ranging rapport. However, we might reasonably say that counsellors should ideally be all-rounders, embodying a good balance of the qualities already mentioned, perhaps especially (and quire rarely) those of emotional intelligence and analytical intelligence combined.

Going even further, it has been said flippantly but challengingly that a counsellor needs the purity of Jesus and the wisdom of Socrates. In other words, in order to rise to the challenge of responding deeply, honestly, creatively and effectively to clients, one would presumably want to embody the best known traits and qualities for helping and transforming lives. Is it an unrealistic perfectionism to aspire to complete honesty and transparency, brilliant rationality and utter integrity? We may say this is fantasy, or that what in fact is most helpful to clients is being 'good enough' and being fallibly human like our clients, rather than heroic or superhuman.

As I have suggested, trainers as interviewers aim to take the best of those who present for training. All being well, trainees are individually given the sort of feedback they need to improve their skills and knowledge, and they will seek whatever therapy and participation in personal development groups that are optimal for their development. Just as counselling is not brain surgery, so counselling training does not have the precision or potency to produce infallibly brilliant counsellors. I have also made the assumption here that training courses as they stand are the inevitable and best means of facilitating effective counsellors.

Further reading

Brear, P., Dorrian, J. & Luscri, G. (2008) Preparing our future counselling professionals: gatekeeping and the implications for research. *Counselling and Psychotherapy Research*, 8 (2), 93–101.

Gilbert, P., Hughes, W. & Dryden, W. (1989) The therapist as a crucial variable in psychotherapy. In W. Dryden & L. Spurling (eds), *On Becoming a Psychotherapist*. London: Tavistock/Routledge.

12

Should Men Counsel?

On the face of it this is an outrageously sexist question. Entry to the counselling profession cannot be limited to women, and clients are both male and female. We would not dare suggest that certain people be excluded based on their ethnicity, religion, sexuality or disability. But we cannot avoid knowing that a majority of trainees and counsellors are women, that over 80 per cent of the BACP membership is female, and that traditionally a majority of clients have been women. The argument that intimacy and emotion are better understood by women is a risky but unavoidable one, and comparisons with caring professions like nursing are also inevitable. Counselling isn't a highly paid career and is often a part-time career, and these again are traditionally female-oriented employment trends. Now, we could avoid this question, or accept that counselling is and may always be a female-'dominated' profession, or we can see what is to be learned from the question.

As in most trusting relationships, it is often men who abuse this trust. Breaches of professional ethics in the priesthood, teaching, law, social work, medicine, and counselling and psychotherapy are often committed more by men than by women. Of course this is not to say that all men are abusive but to recognize that predatory behaviour is more common among men. This seems one good reason to consider reducing risk by excluding all men from intimate professional relationships. Indeed it is the case that some women-only counselling agencies refuse to engage male supervisors. Unfortunately you can add to this line of reasoning the fact that some women seek counselling because they have been abused by men and they frequently prefer women counsellors. And yet this becomes complicated when you consider that some female clients may be specifically helped 'reparatively' by male counsellors, and also when you remember that some men have had unhappy or damaging experiences with female carers. But statistically, men are almost certainly a higher risk.

At a less dramatic level, we should consider the idea that overall men may lack the sensitivity to emotional nuance that is central to counselling. Many feminists have argued that men are as capable of all caring behaviours as women since these are all learned culturally. But others point out that women are biologically built to give birth and to nurture, and some studies suggest that most women are neurologically wired to care, to finely tune into emotions, and that men are quite differently wired. These are contentious views and clearly things are not entirely this black and white. It's highly likely anyway that those men who select themselves for counselling training are more tuned into emotions and interpersonal nuances than most men. But the stubborn fact remains that many of us identify women as more sensitive and, given a choice, a majority of both women and men are likely to say that they would prefer a female counsellor. Some men, for example, will have had as male models in their lives rather uncaring and insensitive men, or will have grown up with the distant, uncommunicative male image.

I think that only a small minority of women would seriously argue for the exclusion of men from counselling practice. Indeed, in my experience many female trainees regret the relative absence of men on their courses. In addition, some men involved in counselling have complained that training and practice may be too female-oriented. Stereotype or not, there is a view that some women over-value 'emotion talk' and under-value or even demean action strategies and intellectuality.

It may be that gender issues should become a more explicit part of counselling training. It must be of some relevance that women suffer more from anxiety, depression, eating disorders, abuse and self-harm, while men are more likely to suffer from anger and violence, alcoholism and suicide. 'Who should men counsel?' or 'Which men should counsel?' may be better questions than 'Should men counsel (at all)?' Which positive qualities are brought to counselling by men? Why is it that, as in so many areas, men predominate in the academic leadership of counselling while they are so under-represented as trainees and practitioners?

It may well be that there are limits to gut-level understanding across genders. For example, one woman who has given birth may understand another's story about a painful birth better than a man can, regardless of his skilful empathy. Similarly, a man devastated by his football team's poor performance may struggle to relate to a female counsellor who thinks it's 'just a game'.

Even more difficult questions may spring from this line of enquiry. Given the liberal commitment of the counselling community to diversity and equal opportunities, there is no reason why a counsellor might not openly be a cross-dresser or transsexual. If it's true that counsellors are more liberal than the general population, some clients are likely to feel uncomfortable with such a counsellor and – where they are offered a choice – may object and express an alternative preference. The liberalism and human rights commitment of (presumably most) counsellors could well clash with a less liberal view. The larger question would then become: 'Who should determine who should counsel whom?'

Further reading

Clare, A. (2000) *On Men: Masculinity in Crisis*. London: Chatto & Windus.
Gross, S. (1995) Revenge of the fathers: incest and the male therapist. *Psychodynamic Counselling*, 1 (2), 263–281.
Rutter, P. (1989) *Sex in the Forbidden Zone: When Men in Power – Therapists, Doctors, Clergy, Teachers and Others – Betray Women's Trust*. London: Mandala.

How Important is the Trainee's Own Personal Therapy?

A great deal of thought has been expended on the question of whether trainees should have personal therapy as part of their training and, if so, how much. In the world of psychoanalytic training this matter is considered so important that objections are simply not entertained, and in some cases trainees must have intensive therapy throughout four or more years of training. Some other institutions insist on personal therapy but are less demanding regarding the amount. Some will insist on a certain minimum, for example 40 hours. The BACP, while requiring a certain amount of personal development work within accredited training courses, have relaxed their original insistence on personal therapy.

Reasons given for such a requirement include the necessity for developing insight and appreciating counter-transference, for learning the training model in depth, for lessening the chance of an unconscious projection of one's own feelings and views on to clients, for a protection against stress, and for understanding what it is like to be in the client's seat. These all seem plausible. Reasons given for doubting the wisdom of such a requirement include the lack of evidence for its need or effectiveness, its coerciveness and cost, its frequent reliance on a list of institute-approved therapists, and a lack of consideration for alternative arrangements.

On the face of it, it seems to make sense that all trainees will have unresolved personal problems or 'material' that will be fruitfully addressed in their own therapy. But this is most obviously relevant in psychoanalytic therapy or psychodynamic counselling where the therapist aims to work with unconscious dynamics. It is less obviously applicable to cognitive behaviour therapy in which the unconscious has no essential part. Some person-centred trainers have suggested that a participation in personal development groups is more fruitful than personal therapy. It isn't possible to require trainees in couple counselling or family therapy to insist on their partners or family members engaging in therapy. Once these perspectives are examined the argument begins to break down.

Perhaps it can be argued that nothing is lost by insisting that trainees have some experience of their own therapy; yet all such therapy costs money in addition to course and supervision costs. Personal training therapy can easily amount to £6,000 or more (at 150 hours at £40 per hour) and critics have suggested that this looks like a pyramid selling scheme. What do you do if you feel that you are not benefiting from this exercise, indeed if you are feeling highly negative about it? Training can be a very expensive commitment and there are reasons for thinking that trainees may go along with therapy that is unhelpful simply in order to protect their financial and career investment. It may be objected that this will be a rare occurrence and that the gains will far outweigh the risks of any losses or dissatisfaction. Indeed it does seem that most trainees report positively on this aspect of their training and it is certainly true that many trainers feel passionately that it is axiomatic that the requirement is necessary and almost certainly beneficial. This remains true even when research fails to justify the belief.

Those therapeutic approaches resting on an assumption that therapy is a lengthy and deep process examining universal neuroses, defences and obstacles of course have a strong point. You would surely not want to license to practise therapeutically someone who refuses to examine their deep unconscious, often negative material. Personal therapy should help to flush these out of their system and enrich their ability to feel deeply, think clearly and live and work effectively. Well, it should – but we don't have hard evidence that it does. Perhaps we should be content with the strong likelihood that it will, even if this is a matter of faith. Even if it is sometimes a fallible procedure, perhaps it is the most plausible route to enhanced effectiveness and a reduced likelihood of perpetrating unconscious damage on clients. Presumably we already have some impressionistic data available comparing trainees who have had extensive personal therapy with those who have had little or none.

I can readily think of practitioners I know, for example, who have had little or no therapy and seem warm and insightful, and some other practitioners who have had a great deal of therapy and seem to lack optimal warmth, insight and other desirable qualities. But overall, we should expect large positive impressions among the extensively 'therapized' compared with others. Such research should not be difficult to organize but I know of none.

Is it 'obvious' that personal therapy must be a training requirement? If so, does its obviousness transcend any need for evidence? Can the outcomes of trainees' own therapy be measured or assessed? Is it self-evidently superior to alternative forms of enhancing trainees' awareness and reducing unconscious blocks and interpersonal deficits? For example, in personal development groups trainees are exposed in their interactions, in their evasions and in their efforts to work on themselves. Might not this be a better form of personal effectiveness enhancement? Of course, it does not duplicate the one-to-one, confidential experience of being a client. In intensive counselling skills training, particularly where trainees use personal material, much is exposed and worked on. Supervision also can often focus on trainees' unresolved or weak areas.

Further reading

Hansen, J.T. (2009) Self-awareness revisited: reconsidering a core value of the counseling profession. *Journal of Counseling and Development*, 87 (2), 186–193.

Macaskill, A. (2000) Personal therapy as a training requirement: the lack of supporting evidence. In C. Feltham (ed.), *Controversies in Psychotherapy and Counselling*. London: Sage.

Masson, J.M. (1990) *Final Analysis: The Making and Unmaking of an Analyst*. London: HarperCollins.

Why Have We Focused on Core Theoretical Models?

A central principle of counselling training – at least for BACP-accredited courses in the UK – is that a core theoretical model (CTM) can be identified and adhered to. The CTM may be any among the full range of psychodynamic, CBT, person-centred, Gestalt, integrative and so on. It is unlikely that an eclectic model would be put forward. The thought behind this view is that students must initially be taught an in-depth coherent model, and later they may choose to add to or modify this training. The CTM should permeate the course. Graduates from such courses should then feel able to demonstrate that they have a basic competency in that approach. All this seems fair enough. There are however some obvious objections.

1   This is not the only sensible way to organize counselling (or psychotherapy) training courses. Other, related professions in the UK and elsewhere do not make this a requirement.
2   Given that there are said to be over 400 different models available, does it make sense to require trainers to arbitrarily deliver any one of these to trainees? The principle of 'It doesn't matter which one you choose but whatever it is, it must be taught thoroughly' hardly seems logical or reassuring, and is unlikely to find favour among the purveyors of NICE guidelines.
3   It is often forgotten that a CTM is just that – a model. It is not fact or hard knowledge. It is a view about how human beings function and malfunction, how certain approaches intervene (technically and relationally), with what rationale, with what limitations. There is little consensus on such matters but if we cared to organize training models around consensus, around common ground, I think we would swing away from arbitrary models towards one generic model.

4 While the existence of hundreds of different models of counselling is colour-
ful and the principle of the BACP or UKCP not favouring one or another seems
democratic, I suspect that we are left with something that is not ultimately
credible. Why not devise an initial, basic consensual training model (common
ethics, relational skills and issues, mental health matters, and a focus on common developmental and emotional problems and cognitive and behavioural
themes and techniques)? Those who choose later to specialize in psychodynamic, Gestalt, existential, psychosynthesis, or other models could do so. But
surely personally preferred therapeutic specialisms should come after funda-
mentals? Personal enthusiasms should not precede agreed common models.

5 Training in and qualification for specific approaches is reflected in service delivery and job opportunities. If you have arbitrarily qualified in, say,
psychodynamic counselling and a relatively rare employment opportunity
arises for a psychodynamic counsellor, all well and good (for *you*). But since
job opportunities in counselling are fairly thin on the ground, wouldn't it
make more sense to organize training around central themes rather than
a large diversity of models with no consensual approval? I know first hand,
for example, how near-impossible job mobility is for counselling academics, when a vacancy at X University is really only open to those from a P
model and another at Y University only to those with a background in a Q
model. This situation is arguably absurd and an example of a closed shop
system. It also means that the public in one geographical area are likely to
have a limited choice that depends on which model that area's university
arbitrarily teaches.

There was probably a sound rationale for having fixed core theoretical
models many years ago but that time has arguably passed, and the indications now are that more generic training models would be appropriate.
The question of CTMs in training is intimately linked with theoretical proliferation and also with employment opportunities. But it will increasingly
link up with NICE guidelines and epidemiology. In other words, when we
can estimate how many people in any given area have certain psychological
problems and needs, we can start to say that certain kinds of training will
have most applicability.

It is quite a different matter to say that you or I have a strong personal
preference or enthusiasm for certain models that we wish to train in. Is there
any good reason why the NHS should endorse such enthusiasms? Underlying
these questions are further problems about the nature of human aspirations,
suffering and the identity of counselling and therapy. For example, psychosynthesis may help some people to explore higher states of consciousness but
it seems currently unlikely that most educational or health institutions will
prioritize their spending on psychosynthesis.

Further reading

Feltham, C. (2000) Against and beyond core theoretical models. In C. Feltham (ed.), *Controversies in Psychotherapy and Counselling*. London: Sage.
Lazarus, A.A. (1990) Can psychotherapists transcend the shackles of their training and superstitions? *Journal of Clinical Psychology*, 46, 351–358.

15

How Much is Theory Related to Practice?

Most counselling training courses contain a fair amount of theory; indeed it is a BACP requirement that they should. On the face of it theory seems obviously necessary to inform and guide trainees and new practitioners. Theories about mental health, the nature of being human, human relationships, psychological problems, the rationale and operation of different interventions – all these seem helpful if not essential. Indeed it is difficult to imagine a theory-free training or practice. Paradoxically, however, many students candidly report that they often find theory, or at least aspects of theory, of little practical use. Those new to practice and in placements often wrestle with the relevance of theory, particularly within sessions themselves. Some who have looked back on their training report that the supervised practice was the most valuable part of their training, perhaps alongside any personal therapy or personal development groups. Sometimes watching competent practitioners counselling (on DVD for example) is also greatly appreciated. Often, in my experience, trainees will question the relevance of any core theory when the moment-by-moment complexity and uniqueness of each therapeutic relationship seems so impossible to fit into a general theory. Also, we should not forget that all theories in our field are somewhat tentative, partial, fluid and developing, and most of them do not hold up strongly when subjected to rigorous tests of validity or evidence of effectiveness.

Theories are formulated in the counselling field in various ways. Most of them have started as the brainchildren of Western men (Freud, Jung, Perls, Berne, Reich, Assagioli, Rogers, Ellis, Beck and others). Some, like Freud's, have come from clinical observation and non-psychology routes; some have been wrought from previous (partially or substantially rejected) theory; and a few have been fairly painstakingly built and modified on the basis of research. Some, frankly, have large elements of inspiration, conjecture and charisma associated with them; some are quite grandiose, claiming an answer for everything; and some are perceived as wild and almost nonsensical. Many clinical theories are faith-like and somewhat hostile to others. Around all these clinical theories we have theoretical input on professional ethics, which is more sober and consensual; mental health or psychiatric matters, which are often contentious and non-consensual; and many others. Theories of human development, for instance – many of them generated and tested by psychology departments – vary enormously in their scope and claims, and practitioners are not always sure how relevant they are. Some theory, such as the social contexts of counselling, is often borrowed and adapted from other disciplines such as sociology.

Given that undistracted attention to the client within each session is paramount, exactly where does the theory come in? It is possible that one has time for micro-hypothesizing and testing out interpretations within sessions but much reflection is done in supervision and at other times outside sessions. Note-taking is one main place where 'clinical' thoughts can be tried out. Sometimes practitioners will read specific client-oriented material.

All in all, it is hard to resist the description of counselling theory as something of a hodge-podge of opinions, beliefs, assertions, clinical-anecdotal observations and semi-academic and academic components. Some courses may have a lot of input on human development and personality while others will have little. And of course, trainees generally commence their placements part-way through a course, when only a certain amount of material has been covered. Course reviews may come up with requests from students to change the sequence of theoretical modules and frankly many would like to be presented with 'everything at once' or instant omniscience. One of the functions of theoretical input may be along the lines of the placebo effect; that is, students come to feel that they know something more than they did and more than the average person does; hence, some degree of confidence may be instilled. Is this a cynical view? Is it what training theory is for?

Asking how much theory is related to practice leads to no solutions but may usefully trigger critical thinking on how we all theorize about counselling. Many are attracted to counselling for its emotional, intuitive and interpersonal aspects, not for its theory. Many trainees prefer short and easy-to-access texts, often case study in type rather than too intellectual. It's quite possible that one can over-theorize or misinterpret but equally possible to be swept away by unreflective emotional currents in counselling practice.

Further reading

Spinelli, E. & Marshall, S. (eds) (2001) *Embodied Theories*. London: Continuum.

16

Are Colleges and Universities the Best Places to Train Counsellors?

Training for counselling in UK academic settings stems from the 1970s and has increased vastly since then but is still not universal and at the time of writing is not required by the BACP. There is nothing unusual about this situation but neither is it inevitable or unquestionable. Having said this, the academicization of counselling training *has* become all but inevitable in this new millennium as part of the move towards statutory regulation. Even those courses in the independent and voluntary sectors commonly seek academic validation. One might therefore suggest that it is pointless to ask this question.

Colleges of further education are natural homes for the kind of vocational training that counsellors need, and growth has occurred at the level of Foundation degrees. But in an uncertain and competitive market overshadowed by imminent statutory regulation, university qualifications often have an edge of perceived superiority, even where the course fees are higher. On the other hand, it is no accident that some traditional universities do not entertain counselling as a subject, unless perhaps as an extramural or lifelong learning course. Psychotherapy has a greater cachet and clinical psychology more still, with the latter requiring doctoral level training and qualifications and therefore needing to be located in or validated by universities. 'Psychoanalytic studies' can be found in some universities, often linked with courses on literature, critical theory and philosophy, but rarely featuring much in psychology courses.

You may be called a cynic if you argue that universities will entertain any subject that promises 'bums on seats' but there is probably some truth in this in an era of higher education having to pay its own way. Note, however, that astrology is not so entertained and complementary and alternative medicine is increasingly challenged in academic settings. Note too that in reaction to changes in government funding and some universities calculating that counselling and psychotherapy courses have relatively small cohorts and do not put quite enough bums on seats, some have closed down such training.

Independent providers of training are often free of institutional encumbrances like heavy-going bureaucracy, ill-fitting modular structures and over-intellectual demands. Counselling focuses to a high degree on the emotional and interpersonal and there is no hard evidence that the ability to pass written assignments, sit exams and make class presentations correlates positively with someone's effectiveness as a counsellor. University accountants prefer large class sizes and often struggle to appreciate the counselling norms of small cohorts and a high level of tutor contact to allow for skills feedback. Universities will provide good library and technological facilities but they will also expect a significant cut from course fees in order to cover such central costs. Perhaps surprisingly, universities cannot always provide teaching and learning accommodation suitable for counselling training, that is, consistent, relatively private and soundproof.

However, small independent training institutions usually cannot command the respect accorded to universities; they cannot, for example, issue their own degrees. Employers are generally more impressed by the latter than the former.

But in the world of counselling and psychotherapy small training providers can often offer better dedicated teaching accommodation, can maintain small class sizes, and have low financial overheads and light, fit-for-purpose bureaucratic systems that allow their staff to concentrate on the necessary teaching, student feedback and maintenance of professional standards. Universities and colleges are sometimes found demoralizing by counselling tutors because teaching demands are heavy and their centralized bureaucracy is burdensome. This situation is sometimes even worse in colleges of further education, with tutors carrying very high teaching (and associated preparation, marking and administrative) loads. Given that counselling is largely about promoting mental health, it isn't rationally consistent to compromise the mental health of tutors by work stress, which is likely to trickle down to students. There is, then, in this argument, serious doubts about universities and colleges being the best places in which to train counsellors.

University and college spokespeople would generally argue that their quality control systems are invaluable and it may be true that small independent training institutions can be compromised by less objective quality control mechanisms. They may not be able to pay their staff as highly, they may succumb to commercial pressures and they may be more tightly and uncritically tied into narrow theoretical traditions. Trite though the point is, it seems that academic and independent trainers each have their pros and cons. To a great extent, how you weigh these factors up depends on larger views about the place of counselling in society and the nature of counselling. If you regard counselling as revolutionary, as being at odds with social norms, then you are likely to hold highly critical views about academic colonization and distortion, and you may agitate for independent training. On the other hand, if you believe that counselling is a predictable health practice like CBT you are likely to want to see it taught and 'quality controlled' in academic settings. However, in an increasingly uncritical, instrumentalist society oriented towards employability rather than critical, political participation and change, universities and colleges seem to be the 'winners' and the independent sector may struggle valiantly to survive.

Further reading

Berry, M. & Woolfe, R. (1997) Teaching counselling in universities: match or mismatch? *British Journal of Guidance and Counselling*, 25 (4), 517–525.

Chiesa, L. (2008) Of teaching and the university discourse. In I. Parker & S. Revelli (eds), *Psychoanalytic Practice and State Regulation*. London: Karnac.

Rizq, R. (2007) On the margins: a psychoanalytic perspective on the location of counselling, psychotherapy and counselling psychology training programmes within universities. *British Journal of Guidance and Counselling*, 35 (3), 283–297.

How Necessary is Psychology to Counselling?

One might assume that an activity and emerging profession like counselling would naturally and essentially belong within psychology, that counsellors would require psychology qualifications. But this is not the case. First, since counselling remains (at the time of writing) a non-statutorily regulated profession, no such requirement exists. Second, no such requirement has ever existed in the UK. Anyone pursuing chartered status as a *counselling psychologist* with the British Psychological Society (BPS) has to have psychology qualifications. But many – perhaps most – counsellors (including myself) will have little or no psychology training or qualifications. Much of this is to do with the fact that many people enter counselling training as mature individuals with other qualifications and as a second or even third career. Historically, it is also related to the fact that psychotherapy and counselling stem from traditions where the founders came from various backgrounds, including neurology, psychiatry, philosophy and psychology. In addition, counselling training has been located in departments of psychology, nursing, social work, pastoral studies and lifelong learning, and in academic, health, business and independent settings.

Since this has been the case for several decades now, one might assume that psychology is *not* necessary. Obviously it is necessary for clinical and counselling psychologists as an intrinsic part of their professional identity. It is, further, possible to argue that psychology *should* form part of counselling training, or that it would be relatively useful. Typical components of psychology awards include research methods, individual differences, social and critical psychology, biological psychology and neuropsychology, memory and language, developmental psychology and evolutionary psychology. It seems clear that some knowledge of different personality traits would be useful, as might a knowledge of human development and lifespan issues, relevant neurology and social psychological dimensions such as power and attraction. Psychology's emphasis on therapists as scientist-practitioners is longstanding and now heavily influences the BACP agenda for training.

Additionally, there are reasons for believing that the academic psychology take on memory clashes with the typical counselling take. For example, a majority of counsellors seem to believe that memories can be retrieved from the very earliest months of life, whereas standard psychological lore is that such memories can go back only to the age of about 4 or 5 (and therefore earlier claims are unreliable or fabricated). But some counselling theory is partly built on such beliefs. Psychologists must be competent statisticians but many counsellors will shy away from statistics, regarding themselves as people-oriented rather than mathematically-oriented. These two traits may co-exist but often do not. Many counsellors believe psychologists to be relatively poor communicators who are overly cognitive, since counselling places quite an emphasis on interpersonal skills and emotion. Psychologists study social psychology but that doesn't necessarily mean they are adept at the practical psychology of relating. The tendency of psychology to aspire to scientific status, and therefore often to draw students from science backgrounds, may underline its professional identity as removed from the more emotional realms of subjectivity, imagination, intuition and empathy.

It is of course telling not only that Freud and psychoanalysis receive minimal attention on psychology courses and are often regarded as anachronistic and unscientific, but also that humanistic psychology is virtually absent from academic psychology courses, and transpersonal psychology is an extremely rare academic commodity. Psychology displays a structural mistrust of intuition, instead relying heavily on (what some consider tedious and unnecessary) an experimental confirmation of the obvious. It is no accident that CBT finds itself at home in psychology departments, where the cognitive is prized and the emotional is usually treated with suspicion. The last statement is incomplete and contentious but worth reflecting on. Some counsellors and psychotherapists have found psychology to be both unnecessary and an obstacle. Certain critical psychologists consider mainstream psychology to be, as it were, in cahoots with capitalism, just as a form of relational psychology finds most psychology uncritically attached to patriarchal values.

Psychology, and indeed other disciplines, may act as correctives against the tendency of some counselling to be drawn towards wild and woolly, ungrounded thinking and practice. It probably does inject some needed rigour into therapeutic outcome claims. It was Hans Eysenck, a psychologist, who drew attention to the lack of empirical evidence in psychotherapy in the 1950s. But the case is far from proven that psychology deserves a *substantial* place in counselling training or practice. Meanwhile, counselling and its ethos exert a critique on psychology, including clinical psychology, as being too detached from the directly and intimately human.

Further reading

van Deurzen-Smith, E. (1993) Does being a psychologist help a counsellor in his or her work? In W. Dryden (ed.), *Questions and Answers for Counselling in Action*. London: Sage.

Parker, I. (2007) *Revolution in Psychology: Alienation to Emancipation*. London: Pluto.

18

How Might Counselling be Expanded as an Academic Subject?

It's possible to be unaware of or uninterested in the status of counselling as an academic subject, although most people will undertake their training in college or university settings and there is an increasing emphasis on counselling as a graduate profession. Counselling is a very small-scale academic subject, a quite recent arrival on the academic scene (from the 1970s in the UK) and can be found in diverse settings such as (alongside or within) psychology, social work, theology and lifelong learning. Counselling is an applied subject – that is, it concerns itself with a clinical, pastoral or interpersonal practice of helping or enquiry. In this it resembles nursing but it has evolved largely in non-medical settings. Its curriculum contains a great deal of skills practice, personal development work and closely supervised placement work. Those elements drawing from a substantive knowledge base include a study of key figures and movements (e.g. Freud, Jung, Rogers, Beck and their therapeutic theories); theories of human development; social contexts of counselling; mental health; professional, ethical and legal issues; and research methods. There is no requirement that psychology be included as such; indeed counselling psychology is developing separately, and counselling is dwarfed by psychology in terms of its popularity and recruitment figures. Much of this has to do with counselling still being an emerging and small-scale profession.

Counselling (even if we include psychotherapy and its 100-year-old history) does not possess the weight of the natural sciences. James D. Watson famously claimed that 'Physics is the only science – the rest is just social work', so we can guess what he would say about counselling. Nor does it have the gravitas of the social sciences, arts and humanities subjects. It has a greater similarity to management studies in terms of its recency and applied nature (although not in terms of its income generation capacity). Some might say that it resembles drama studies insofar as it has a focus on the emotional and its graduates face uncertain careers. Some regard it as being aligned with complementary and alternative medicine, often with dubious associations of unprovenness. And some might rank it in terms of reputation with leisure studies, media studies and women's studies, implying (rightly or wrongly) a lack of academic weight and rigour. We may be content with this state of affairs, accepting that counselling will never have the power, kudos and pulling power of more traditional and 'sexier' subjects.

Arguably counselling is about what is most human about us – our individual subjectivity – and in this it resembles the tradition of English literature with its focus on human narrative and interiority. Originally psychology focused via introspection on the subtleties of our mental processes but lost this focus in its anxiety to be regarded as scientific, dealing only with the measurable. Insofar as counselling is about the human need for meaning and purpose, philosophy and theology originally met this need but are both now found to be too abstruse for a majority of people. Sociology, cultural studies and psychoanalytic studies may to some extent fill this need but are once again often experienced as highly abstruse.

It may be the very raw, personal, emotional, subjective and universal nature of the subject matter that renders counselling unlikely to achieve greater academic status. It could even be argued that counselling and its focus on the most highly personal should not become academicized. Perhaps humanistic psychology comes closest to honouring what is most human within us but humanistic psychology is not found in many British academic settings. Anthropology – the study of human beings – perhaps ought to be the place where counselling finds an academic home, yet anthropology too has become a highly specialized subject to which many find it hard to relate.

Here is a suggestion. Given the importance of examining the human condition, looking at human nature and human potential in all its aspects, why can we not see academic disciplines as intersecting at the human? A certain amount of traditional psychology, philosophy, sociology, politics and literature could be retained but we might add those aspects of evolution and history that help to explain human behaviour in all its stubbornness. Current affairs and trends should also be factored in, along with a 'local knowledge' that is relevant to actual students. We might also include studies of the transhuman or posthuman to enable us to consider what kind of future is optimal. But we can go even further than this by fully honouring human subjectivity. Personal development groups could be used to examine links between *unique* human motivations and behaviours with wider social theories. In this way knowledge can become both objective and subjective, and relevant to human beings at the human level. At the moment, in spite of a fair level of interest in counselling, students and counsellors do not seem to have the confidence or hunger to push for such an expanded subject and it may be that, as with CBT, most people have bought into the instrumentalist notions of academia-for-employability and studying for transferable skills' sake rather than an interest in the deep human condition.

Further reading

Thorne, B. & Dryden, W. (eds) (1993) *Counselling: Interdisciplinary Perspectives*. Milton Keynes: Open University Press.

Training and Curriculum Issues:

Challenge

Whose responsibility and right is it to decide on matters of training? Traditionally we tend to accept (sometimes have to accept) what professional bodies, educational institutions and tutors say, and we may have little or no choice. But McAuliffe and Erikson (2000) argue for a re-imagining of training, with a shift towards co-constructed features. On considering each of the sections within this group of topics, where would you go for further clarification? Has research answered any of these questions conclusively? Insofar as you may hold views of your own that are critical of conventional training, what are the obstacles to taking these further? Who among the stakeholders opposes change and on what grounds?

Further reading

McAuliffe, G. & Eriksen, K. (2000) *Preparing Counselors and Therapists: Creating Constructivist and Developmental Programs.* Virginia Beach, VA: Donning.

Case Study

Gill is doing a Master's in psychotherapy at an independent training institute. It has cost her a great deal of money already. On submitting her thesis she is told it is not yet suitably pitched or ready and that she should take at least another year. But she will have to pay another year's fees. The institute operates on an autocratic, expert knowledge basis and, in spite of the MA being validated by a university, has no clear published assessment criteria. Gill is afraid that if she complains she may suffer, and she can't afford to sacrifice her heavy investment in the course. What ethical and educational principles may be involved here and what would your thinking and decisional process be if you were in Gill's position? (See Safouan, 2000.)

Critical thinking perspectives

On the face of it, we might say that stringent university bureaucracy procedures are critical tools for ensuring quality control in just such situations (see du Gay, 2000). In other words, we might regard colleges and universities as conservative bodies requiring critique but we should also look at the opposite case. Perhaps just as there are pressure groups arguing for alternative, religiously-based universities (opposed to the secular assumptions of most universities), so we should perhaps retain a vigorous independent sector for psychotherapy training. We can also go further and argue that psychotherapy and counselling training essentially needs no seal of approval from the state education system. Is there a risk of deadening bureaucracy at one extreme and unaccountable charismatic authoritarianism on the other? Should Gill be regarded as an unwitting consumer or is she also responsible for which course she joins and who she confronts? Is there necessarily any relation between courses and who delivers them, and the ultimate impact on clients?

Theories of Counselling Practice

Who Founds Schools of
Counselling and Why?

By 'schools' I mean distinctly named approaches, orientations, brands. In this field, usually under the heading of psychotherapy rather than counselling, a single founding figure can often be identified. Usually that figure is a male, often a 'dead white male'. Usually it has been a male from Europe or North America. Frequently these figures have been Jewish (Freud, Adler, Reich, Perls, Berne, Frankl, Wolpe, Ellis, Beck, Mahrer, et al.), although we can think of some who don't fit this template gender-wise (e.g. Anna Freud, Melanie Klein, Laura Perls, Insoo Kim Berg, Marsha Linehan, and Francine Shapiro), and religiously or culturally (Jung, Rogers). But overwhelmingly these are the 'founding fathers' of psychotherapy and counselling. Often referred to as charismatic, I'm not sure what evidence there is of such charisma but certainly most have been intellectuals, writers, and independent thinkers. Many approaches were born out of a frustration with or a rejection of previous approaches, often accompanied by personal rifts with colleagues or academic or professional establishments. Few counselling traditions have been created by a committee or painstaking research.

These observations may or may not seem important but I suspect they are very relevant for thinking about the nature of counselling. The Jewish male connection may not mean anything other than that there is strong intellectual tradition in Judaism and a patriarchal (and white) tradition in academia, medicine and related professions. But since a majority of British counsellors are female and much of the content of counselling is about the interpersonal, communicative and emotional, we might expect to see a greater female presence among founders and writers. Indeed we do of course see some of this in the feminist therapy movement, with key figures like Jean Baker Miller, Susie

Orbach and Carol Gilligan. But why is the field still so dominated by white male figures, and what influence must this have?

We might note that the same holds true in philosophy and religion. Prolific, opinionated white male intellectuals restlessly argue among themselves and create new systems and schools of thought all the time. We do not know to what extent these founders self-consciously want to be founders, important, influential, with followers, nor whether their motives are mainly intellectual, creative, altruistic, commercial or otherwise. Some may simply be following their own interests and convictions while others perhaps harbour less noble motives to become famous, immortal, wealthy and so on. We may ask why counselling should be any different from other fields of endeavour. Scientists often compete furiously for recognition and awards, for example, just as politicians strive to make their name, wield influence and 'leave a legacy'. Perhaps all this doesn't sit quite right within counselling, which aims to be at least somewhat non-neurotic and altruistic. Or perhaps many male founders think like engineers, striving to solve what they see as problems and coming up with new (theoretical and technical) inventions to address these problems?

There is surely some link between the proliferation of schools of therapy and the founder figures we are discussing here, and also a link with the failure of the integrative ideal to mature. If, instead of carving out illustrious careers and reputations for themselves, these men collaborated (with women too!), might not more progress be made? Might we not address more helpfully the need for a theory and practice for understanding and reducing individual human distress?

Another perspective on this is the possibility that the best or most human therapeutic work, and perhaps the least fêted, is the quietly conducted everyday practice of the 'unknown counsellor', perhaps often a woman? Do male theorists grab the headlines while female workers quietly do the bulk of the real work? I have considered elsewhere the place and useful extent of theory and we might speculate that it is over-rated. Just as male theorists may be academically dominant even in the fields of obstetrics, childcare and human development, women remain the primary hands-on workers in these areas. However, when I have discussed these issues with female students and colleagues there has often been some excitement about the prospect of creative thinking, writing and research. There is a desire to create new ideas and guides to counselling practice but perhaps insufficient time and confidence.

We also need to ask why counselling theory has not been more or better informed by non-Judeo-Christian traditions and from outside of Europe and

North America. Or we might also recognize that most counselling theory and practice is more geographically limited than we imagine. In addition, posterity may look back and see clearly the links between the founders of therapeutic approaches, the conditions of the West in the twentieth century, and the other ways in which individual problems in living were addressed throughout the world.

Further reading

Feltham, C. (ed.) (1997) *Which Psychotherapy? Leading Exponents Explain Their Differences.* London: Sage.

Which Theories of Human Development are Most Relevant in Counselling Training and Practice?

Most courses will contain some input on theories about the development of human psychological functioning and dysfunction. Infant observation is an important part of some psychoanalytic training, for example, and the theories of Freud, Klein, Bowlby and Winnicott about the early development of mental functioning and relationships with caregivers are generally influential. According to some theorists it is precisely this (sometimes highly speculative, sometimes empirically evidenced) focus on very early development that has created dissatisfaction and led to new theories. For example, Jung wanted to stress the equal importance of development and choice in midlife and later life. Developmental psychology itself was slow to acknowledge that development occurs well beyond the traditional focus on early years and adolescence, and that it doesn't occur uniformly and in a social vacuum. Logically, less interest has been shown in human development by tutors and practitioners in CBT, solution-focused therapy and brief therapies. With the increase in transpersonal and multicultural therapy models, questions about reincarnation and karma also increase. Some communities believe that the past co-exists with the present, and some regard the past as being in front of them, with the future being behind. Indeed, the more closely one examines the curricular choice of what to include, the more problematic and fascinating it becomes.

What would constitute a comprehensive list of topics for a module in therapeutically relevant human development? Consider the following possible ingredients and which seem most and least relevant to you and your practice needs. We might look at human genetic and evolutionary development; the concept of reincarnation and past-lives therapy; transgenerational theories and therapy; intra-uterine experience; early neurological development; critical periods; birth, birth trauma and related therapies; attachment and object relations theories; physical, emotional and cognitive development; personality type development; the influences of gender, race, sexuality, culture, class, education, religion, nutrition, physical characteristics, life chances and accidents on development; losses, abuses and traumas across the lifespan; major decisions and changes; idiosyncratic life paths; local, national and global events and their impacts; career and economic factors; family and relationship factors; ageing in all its facets; disability, illness, dying and death; concepts of posthumous existence.

My guess is that some of these suggestions will be readily seized upon and some summarily dismissed by various readers on the grounds of perceived irrelevance, credibility, unprovenness, prejudice and so on. Note that psychologists are generally taught, and teach, that we have no reliable memory for anything before the age of about 4 or 5 – an assertion that is flatly denied by many therapists. Given the sheer diversity of clients, it is quite likely that clients can potentially present issues related to any of these matters whether or not the counsellor has much knowledge of or belief in them. Many counsellors will have examined such diversity in their own therapy or personal development groups but primarily in experiential and narrative terms rather than with theoretical rigour. Across the 400 or so different models of counselling, some (e.g. hypno-regressive therapy) take past lives as a fact and as therapeutically rich material, some will focus hard on birth trauma and the re-experiencing of birth, while others will consider these to be examples of superstitious, unproven beliefs and dangerous nonsense. CBT therapists may sometimes try to elicit the origins of their clients' cognitive schemas, that is, when certain chronic, automatic, negative thoughts emerged and how they were reinforced. And some, such as solution-focused therapists, may refer to the past only to elicit clients' previous exercising of strengths and successes.

Courses designed around specific models will probably exclude many of the above possibilities. An imaginary comprehensive course could include them all. But we would still need to ask what their relevance is to counselling practice. They would certainly make us better equipped to understand the beliefs of a wider multicultural community. They are likely to equip us better to work with clients from the full lifespan. They might also alert us better to identifying sources of distress that would otherwise be overlooked, and in some cases to possible ways of working that we wouldn't normally embrace, or to the need to refer on. But barriers would still remain. How would you respond to a client who persists in the belief that his problem is rooted in a past life and that only by accessing a memory of that past life can he resolve the problem? Would you learn and duly attempt to offer a hypno-regressive technique? Would you refer him on? Or would you pathologize his belief or simply tell him that you cannot help him? Indeed his belief might be 'pathological', a defence against unconscious conflict or pain. Or he might simply be mistaken. Or you might be limited in what you can allow yourself to believe, based on your temperament and/or your training. Actually there is nothing strange about any of this, since the field of human development as an academic discipline itself cannot claim any consensus.

We also have the problem that all such theories of human development generalize. They cannot tell us exactly how each operates in the life of every individual client. Of course it would be weirdly omniscient if any theory, technique or instrument could map out precisely all the sources of individual distress (although the human genome project attempts to do something of this sort). In clinical practice the practitioner does her or his best, based on experience and sometimes using diagnostic means, to help clients identify specific causes of distress. But even then we must face the question of quite what to do with such information.

Further reading

Harris, J.R. (2006) *No Two Alike: Human Nature and Human Individuality*. New York: Norton.

Kagan, J. & Snidman, N. (2004) *The Long Shadow of Temperament*. Cambridge, MA: Belknap.

Thomas, R.M. (1999) *Human Development Theories*. Thousand Oaks, CA: Sage.

How do Genes, Personality, Object Relations and Life Events Interact?

Many humanistic counsellors do not think in terms of genetic influences or personality traits but most counsellors seem to wrestle somewhat with the interplay of factors that lie within each of their clients and inform progress and obstacles to progress. It is possible to think of the client purely in the here and now, as a free agent reporting on the flow of his thoughts and feelings, but quite often part of client narratives and of what counsellors hear for themselves arouses curiosity about other aspects of the person.

Genes are by no means fully comprehended and certainly not understood by most counsellors but few can deny that many of us look physically like one of our parents and often have habits and traits that resemble family members'. Many would acknowledge that to an extent schizophrenia, bipolar disorder and obsessive compulsive disorder 'run in families'. It's also been suggested that many subclinical traits operate similarly. Parents frequently observe that out of two or three of their children, each is different in ways that do not seem dependent on their child-rearing practices; many will say, 'He was born like it, he's always been the same'. It may be that since quite a lot of counselling theory arose in 'psychodynamic times' and among humanistic thinkers problems were often located in parenting styles, but now there is more willingness perhaps to take in other influences. Advances in genetic research suggest that many of our behaviours may be more deeply rooted in our biology than we thought, or than we like to think. One huge problem for counselling here is that this challenges beliefs in the causes of (and hence solutions for) personal problems lying in the counselling-accessible territory of (recalled) childhood.

Not all would agree but personality factors such as introversion and extraversion, and optimism and pessimism, appear relatively evident and somewhat fixed rather than chosen or strongly modifiable. Psychology's classical 'Big 5' personality traits are openness, conscientiousness, extraversion, agreeableness and neuroticism, and again we may readily observe these (or their opposites) at work. Individuals will appear to bear certain traits quite strongly and persistently. There are many alternative schemes which include individuals' orientation to different learning domains in affect, cognition and behaviour, for example, or in verbal, spatial, social, artistic or practical domains. The key point is that some of us are strongly oriented in ways that may help or hinder progress in counselling. These characteristics probably have strong genetic associations but alternative rationales do exist, most challengingly those based on past-lives theory.

Object relations are familiar to most counsellors even when they do not belong in the psychodynamic tradition. All of us must negotiate our way through the earliest years with parents of variable lovingness, skill and reliability. The interplay between the infant's innate characteristics and needs and the caregiver's qualities, the subtle nuances of early relationships, can be powerful features in how we develop. Whatever genetic characteristics we have, we may thrive or fragment according to our early relational history. Often the most damaged individuals have had the least consistent and most traumatic of childhoods, for example being erratically parented, abandoned, brought up haphazardly in care systems, fostered and adopted.

Another major area for client narratives and counsellor assessment is life events. Whether we are talking about key early events (subtle or dramatic) remembered as significant, or outstanding traumas, or clusters of challenging events, it seems certain that often such events represent crises, tests of resilience and turning points. Sometimes simply to recall these and put them in perspective and to experience some catharsis is enough. Sometimes the way in which clients cope with such events is influenced by innate and early life factors, and psychodynamic counsellors in particular trace such trains of association and their manifestation in transference. CBT therapists too may sometimes trace current thinking patterns back to early life schemas.

Clearly some therapeutic approaches do not rest on making links with past events or genetic clues, but they do often implicitly assume clients' basic resilience or ready capacity for learning and behavioural change. This may be a major reason for such therapies not always working effectively, that is, because not all individuals can easily move on if they have previous pertinent deficits. Issues of this kind should perhaps feature in all courses, even where the core model minimizes attention to them. One need not agree about their equal importance but it would seem remiss not to ask whether these factors might underpin a therapeutic failure or if paying attention to them might sometimes enhance progress. In the case of strong claims to genetic influence, disagreement in itself can prove stimulating.

Further reading

Cramer, D. (1992) *Personality and Psychotherapy.* Milton Keynes: Open University Press.
Douthit, K.Z. (2006) The convergence of counseling and psychiatric genetics. *Journal of Counseling and Development,* 84 (1), 16–28.
Rutter, M. (2006) *Genes and Behavior: Nature-Nurture Interplay Explained.* Malden, MA: Blackwell.

22

What Roles do Chance, Destiny and Control Play in our Lives?

This question can be phrased in many ways. On the one hand we can see ourselves as wholly contingent and accidental: 'A million million spermatozoa, but the one was me', wrote Aldous Huxley. If your mother and father hadn't met, you wouldn't exist. If you hadn't been born where you were, you would have embraced a different religion. If you had been born to different parents and into a different class you *might* be more intelligent, richer or advantaged in other ways. If you hadn't worked at a certain workplace you wouldn't have met your partner (the love of your life), nor would your particular children have existed. If you hadn't been driving your car on that road that night you wouldn't have had that terrible accident. We could equally insist that these were all destined by God or fate and that whatever the case, it is in the way we embrace and work with our circumstances that we own and shape our lives. We can disregard such questions and take an existentialist view that we are simply here, free to choose our own courses of action. Or perhaps in some subtle way we could argue that these are all aspects of the same dynamic: we are all that we are.

If I had not been born into a working-class family and been a shy introvert perhaps I would have been more confident and progressed better in life. If I had not passed my 11-plus exam and gone to grammar school, perhaps I would have had a wholly different career experience. If I had not read Janov's *The Primal Scream* in 1973 and subsequently gone to Los Angeles for that therapy, perhaps I would not have become interested in therapy at all. If Windy Dryden had not been my tutor at Aston University in 1980 I might never have found my way into writing for publication. I could multiply these personal examples but the point of course is that my life might have been very different but for a range of biological, social and educational factors. If I had been a bit more depressed than I was around the age of 20, perhaps I might have killed myself. If I had not had some mysterious driving force to think and write I might not be a professor today. I say 'mysterious' because there was nothing of this kind of thing anywhere in my family background. On the other hand, had I been born earlier, or in another class, I might have become a professor in another university, with ample time in which to think and write and with minimal bureaucracy! There is both an 'It's all academic' refrain and a 'There but for the grace of God' undertow to all this, for all of us. Things could have been better or worse, and they certainly are better and worse for many others.

The point is – we have to work with what we have. Clients (ourselves in the other chair) have their own constellations of chance, destiny and control factors. Some appear to possess an heroic resolve, overcoming monstrous odds to thrive. Others may appear ambivalent or resistant, denying that they can change anything. Quite often we admire the former and feel frustrated with the latter. Sometimes a counsellor will confess that she wishes she had the energy or resolve of her client. But this subtlety of individual differences may have more involved in it than a mere refusal to take responsibility. At least one argument here, from the literature on primal therapy, is that we are born differently, with some of us experiencing a successful, 'natural' transition from womb to world, but others experiencing immense and sometimes life-threatening obstacles. If true, this means that the former may experience all subsequent life as welcoming and benign, with attendant virtuous circle consequences, while the latter may experience all life as frustrating, difficult and unrewarding (without the appropriate therapy). It's your good luck to be in the first group. Variations on this theme exist, so that if you are lucky to experience particularly benign object relations you are more likely to thrive in life.

In certain radical humanistic theories we are all held to be responsible for all that happens to us, however apparently accidental or catastrophic, including rape and other forms of violence (Schutz, 1979). Hardly fair – but life isn't fair, in such theories. Of course, anyone might be born well but somehow run into accidents or a series of misfortunes, and the balance could be tilted away from the original 'setting' (e.g. the pauper unexpectedly meets a millionaire and marries him, or the millionaire has a terrible accident). Some who seem to 'have everything' can appear to sabotage their own chances of a successful life for no apparent reason at all.

Most of us would agree perhaps on the wisdom of accepting the hand of cards we are born with (rather than railing against it) and playing it as well as we can. Some would deny that there is any such chance element – that human will is supreme and available to us all. Most models of counselling will offer explanations for why things go awry and how we can take control in re-authoring our lives. Re-decision therapy is one of these. Unfortunately there is a quite common tendency to imply a linearity in therapeutic change rather than acknowledging that to an extent our lives are probably mired in chaos and that, as a result, our therapeutic progress is also often nonlinear. We may generally improve our good chances by taking more control over our lives (exercise and sensible eating are likely to forestall heart attacks) but unfortunately not even the most positive client can avoid the freak accident waiting to happen. Meanwhile, is it fair to critique much counselling and psychotherapy training for emphasizing certain patterns of behaviour and implying that therapeutic change may be reasonably predictable?

Further reading

Bussolari, C.J. & Goodell, J.A. (2009) Chaos theory as a model for life transitions counseling: nonlinear dynamics and life's changes. *Journal of Counseling and Development*, 87 (1), 98–107.
Chamberlain, L.L. & Butz, M.R. (eds) (1998) *Clinical Chaos: A Therapist's Guide to Nonlinear Dynamics and Therapeutic Change*. Philadelphia, PA: Brunner/ Mazel.

What's Wrong with Psychoanalytic Therapy?

First, a word about names: there are many forms of psychoanalytically derived therapy and counselling, and many different names attaching to these. In some cases real differences do exist, indeed to the point of conflict. However, for the purposes of this section I will attempt to treat them as one, or rather to address their common features and problems.

Virtually all such therapy is focused on ideas of unconscious processes distorting our ability to lead satisfactory lives, and on the task of therapy being to uncover unconscious conflicts through the medium of the intense therapeutic relationship. Working through, transference, interpretation and insight are all key features. At the core of this view is the tenet of self-deception which dictates that our conscious processes are often insufficiently clear for us to lead optimal lives in the domains of love and work. Therapists must themselves have intensive training that includes *deep* personal training therapy that itself frees them significantly from unconscious conflict. This enables psychoanalysts, psycho-analytic psychotherapists and psychodynamic counsellors to work patiently and skilfully with transference, with high levels of awareness of their own countertransference. Psychoanalytic therapy is a depth process taking a great deal of time, but aims to free patients or clients from complex layers of self-deception and destructive repetitive patterns of thinking, feeling and behaviour. Many therapists aligned with this way of working are themselves critical of the claims of other therapies.

The psychoanalytic models being the oldest in the field, the various critiques (and critics) are probably well known:

1   There is little evidence for the reality of an 'unconscious' and the other psy-choanalytic constructs posited in relation to mental apparatus. Likewise regarding transference. Indeed many find the language and concepts of psychoanalysis vague, impenetrable and obfuscating. There is an accom-panying problem of perception that psychoanalysts interpret everything in terms of a pathologizing 'secret code' of the unconscious.

2   There is relatively little objective evidence of successful outcomes and, with the therapeutic process usually being so protracted, many complicating variables (such as the passage of time and the criteria for assessing an out-come) exist that make evaluation extremely difficult. However, as the long-est established therapy, one might expect to see at least greater anecdotal evidence of successful analysands.

3   Such therapy insists that all presenting symptoms have deep underly-ing structures linked with family and early interpersonal (object relations) conflicts – but there is much competing evidence that many personal prob-lems have their origins in genetic, social learning and adult experience, with suggestive remedies lying closer to the present or in psychopharmacology.

4   A great deal of the psychoanalytic enterprise rests on faith in the expertise and the integrity of the practitioner, yet critics like Masson (1992) have argued that analysts can be as incompetent, neurotic and abusive as anyone else.

5   The required length and intensity of psychoanalytic treatment mean that patients must spend a great deal of money without necessarily seeing any sign of obvious improvement, often becoming dependent on the therapist in the process. In addition, some will continue on the 'sunk costs' principle – 'I don't feel any better but now I've come this far and spent this much, I'd bet-ter carry on'. This is a little like regular lottery participants who feel, super-stitiously, that they have to keep going with the same numbers in case the big win is just around the corner.

6   The length and non-specific aims and outcomes of these therapies mean that they are usually available only 'privately' to those affluent enough to afford them, and the NHS is unlikely to endorse them.

7 According to many critics, psychoanalysis is an anachronistic belief system with weak clinical outcomes, and while its theories may have some attractions (for example in interpreting literature), overall it is more a philosophy than a validated psychological science or treatment.

8 Given its nineteenth-century origins and Freud's scientific aspirations, it is no surprise (but probably an indictment) that psychoanalysis incorporates little in the way of modern evolutionary and genetic knowledge, nor of neurology, sociology and so on. Indeed its original theories of psychosomatic aetiology and cure, some of which still persist, are considered dangerously anti-scientific by many.

9 The central claim of psychoanalytic thought – that our unconscious conflicts and defences prevent us from spontaneously recovering or from being capable of rational action – seems to lead to a determinism that is not credible.

10 The history of psychoanalysis is littered with in-fighting and schisms that continue into the present, as can be witnessed in splits between the UKCP, the British Psychoanalytic Council, the College of Psychoanalysts, and so on.

11 Many founders of humanistic and CBT approaches rejected their own psychoanalytic backgrounds because they found such practice too slow and indeterminate. But in addition many would criticize psychoanalytic therapies for their relative neglect of raw emotion, the reality of the body, and interpersonal authenticity.

It is no secret that some critics have referred to psychoanalysis as a hoax, that most academic psychologists tend to regard it as of historical interest only, and that it seems to survive (in the UK) mainly as a private enterprise for the affluent in places like North London and partly as an object of fascination for some philosophers, critical theorists, feminists and artists. It remains highly regarded in France (especially in its Lacanian form) but has recently been downgraded in Sweden. It has certainly been a rich source of hypotheses about mental functioning and there are some weak indications of its vindication by neuroscience. Personally, I agree absolutely that human beings are given to self-deception and deception of each other, both individually and systemically, but we don't need psychoanalysis to tell us this. Nor can psychoanalysis deliver us from this volume of deception.

Overall, any judgement on the utility and value of psychoanalytic theories and practice leans towards the frankly sceptical, in spite of its historical radicalism and beguiling interpretations. But we could also argue that our worldviews and judgements always stem from our personalities, including their unconscious conflicts, and that if we all underwent psychoanalysis we might appreciate its value.

Further reading

Crewes, F. (ed.) (1988) *Unauthorized Freud: Doubters Confront a Legend*. New York: Penguin.
Webster, R. (1995) *Why Freud Was Wrong*. London: HarperCollins.

What Are the Limitations of the Person-centred Approach?

The person-centred approach – still very much the 'brainchild' of Carl Rogers – remains one of the most popular of counselling and psychotherapy approaches in the UK. This is probably due to its positive view of human nature and potential and also to its relative simplicity in the marketplace of often complicated theories. Adherents of the PCA point out that it is often misunderstood as something simplistic and is often caricatured rather than fully explored. I think they would agree that it rests on the belief that human nature, however complex, is fundamentally trustworthy and directed towards prosocial ends – and that its therapy is capable of restoring self-acceptance and empowerment to its clients via a deeply intimate and skilled relationship. As perhaps the pre-eminent humanistic model, it promotes the view that we are trustworthy in our feelings and intentions and that attention must be directed to the core of each person and his or her actualizing tendency, to the client's own inner meanings and feelings. In this sense the PCA is countercultural, valuing the person above socioeconomic ends or fashions and above medical and psychiatric assumptions.

What are the possible limitations of the PCA? I list them here (drawn from well-known but diverse sources of criticism) in no particular order:

1   The PCA shows insufficient interest in the complexity of human beings, including their evolved nature, sometimes evil propensities and aggressive and greedy features.
2   The PCA predicts, indeed insists, that all clients regardless of the nature, depth or complexity of their personal problems, are best helped by the PCA faith in their own resources and the therapeutic relationship rather than by any technical interventions.
3   The PCA offers relatively little objective evidence of its effectiveness, relying rather on faith and case studies.
4   The PCA shows little if any awareness of the countervailing forces upon clients, so that whatever gains they may make during therapy within an acceptant environment may well be susceptible to erosion in the real world of stress, work, family, community, illness and so on.
5   The PCA remains relatively naïve about the costs of therapy, so that time limits are logically necessary rather than allowing the individual client to dictate how long he or she wishes to continue.
6   The PCA may nod in the direction of unconscious or self-deceptive processes and the need for setting behavioural goals, but essentially it takes what clients say at face value and allows them to talk indefinitely (i.e. without therapist-suggested actions).
7   The precise meaning of 'person-centred' is confused. It refers to a belief that everything must come back to the individual person and her or his feelings, thoughts and decisions. But often clients are asking for an intervention from someone who might be aware of something better for them than their own indirect, hit or miss route.
8   The PCA practitioner, while presenting her or his views as deeply held personal tenets, is unlikely to see clients free of charge and also unlikely to extend person-centred conditions to everyone in her or his everyday life.

I am aware that some items on this list will be objected to as inaccurate. Let me take and unpack the first – we are evolved, we have a partly genetically determined nature, some of us have somewhat evil or psychopathic traits and many if not most of us contain, propagate and acquiesce in selfish, harmful, greedy, aggressive, deceptive behaviours that are common in society. We may also have some 'good' traits alongside these but it is hard to see how our less noble traits stem from (largely parental) 'conditions of worth' which are relatively easily overturned. One will search in vain for references to Darwin in Rogers' writings and most diehard person-centred practitioners will argue that humans have large resources of freedom and self-determination. You have only to observe someone in the throes of a stubborn obsessive compulsive episode to see that such behaviour is not freely chosen, is not derived from conditions of worth and is rarely overturned by any amount of therapeutic conditions like warmth and empathy.

PCA theorists seem routinely to make an overstatement about the scope of self-determination that is barely credible.

Is all the power necessary for change already within each person? This seems to be a claim of PCA practitioners. No nudges or techniques are necessary for any client, given enough time and persistence and skill with core therapeutic conditions. Whether you are experiencing post-traumatic stress, nicotine addiction, bipolar disorder or anorexia (and PCA 'diehards' will eschew all such diagnostic terms anyway), the application of PCA principles will give clients what they need. It may take longer, they may not even resolve such problems, but they will in time accept themselves and find therapeutic satisfaction; and, having found their own way there (albeit with a PCA companion), they are then likely to have learned some sort of valuable meta-lesson in self-trust along the lines of teaching someone to fish rather than giving him fish. In such a belief, it seems to me, there is strong possibility of time-wasting and inefficiency, not to mention in protracting the client's suffering, in the interests of sticking dogmatically with a PCA core tenet.

Further reading

Wilkins, P. (2003) *Person-Centred Therapy in Focus.* London: Sage.

25

What's Wrong with CBT?

Many distinct schools of behaviour therapy and cognitive therapy still exist but almost by default the merger into cognitive behaviour therapy (CBT) has taken centre stage. The key principle of CBT is that we are not hapless victims of what happens to us, we are not at the mercy of our emotions; rather, almost everything that goes on around us, that happens to us or that courses through our feelings, is mediated by our thoughts. Our 'negative automatic thoughts' and the negative behaviours that accompany them create or reinforce unhelpful feelings and physiological reactions. We have some tendency to evaluate personal events (past, present and future) incorrectly. Negative, depressogenic thinking, for example, clearly exacerbates any depressive tendencies. A chain of thoughts that ratchets up the chances of things going wrong or becoming catastrophic in a forthcoming personal challenge increases the odds of failure and further self-recrimination. Avoidant behaviour tends to lead to greater anxiety and further avoidance. The basic rationale for CBT – stemming from ancient Greek stoical tenets – is well known, and of course the theory is much more complicated than this. Techniques, including thought diaries, homework and in-session disputation, abound. Above all, we are told that copious research supports the claims of CBT's effectiveness far above those of competing therapies.

Hence, we now see an expansion of CBT from its original application to depression and anxiety to many other conditions. CBT is usually quite short term, fits into NHS circumstances well and is associated with client-friendly commonsense values. We see it being promoted by the National Institute for Health and Clinical Excellence (NICE) for many conditions, funded by government and touted as making major inroads on the nation's mental health problems. We also see its renewed attention to the subtleties of the therapeutic relationship, to mindfulness, compassion and other topics. Almost everyone I know in professional counselling and psychotherapy circles would agree that CBT has something positive to offer.

However, serious reservations about CBT have been put forward but are rarely dealt with. These include the following:

1 There is no conclusive evidence that most humans are primarily cognitive beings, that all humans can use cognitive control to manage and change difficult feelings and behaviours. Despite the inclusion of affect in the title of rational *emotive* behaviour therapy (REBT), it seems clear that CBT values thought and behaviour above feelings, contra many humanistic therapies .

2 It has been argued by all psychoanalytic and many humanistic practitioners that CBT's primary focus on the client's present and on the control of feelings, along with its relatively short-term delivery, cheat clients of a thorough therapeutic opportunity and that its symptomatic focus is largely suppressive.

3   CBT's emphasis on assessment (or case formulation), its use of evaluation instruments and frequent written homework assignments are found off-putting by many clients, creates a barrier between client and therapist and leads to outward compliance, false records of success and the suppression of complex or painful client material.

4   Anecdotally many colleagues nationally have reported waiting lists for CBT in the NHS to be around a year or two, with some stories of clients being told on assessment that they are 'too depressed' or 'not compliant'. If true, evaluations of CBT success would be skewed by such practices. Anecdotal evidence, while unreliable, should also not be simply brushed aside.

5   Along with many colleagues in a variety of settings and parts of the country, I have heard client reports of unsuccessful CBT. Indeed I know some of these cases quite intimately. I have heard of clients feeling pressurized to comply with CBT paperwork and homework that they were uncomfortable with or had reservations about. Nevertheless their therapy may be officially recorded as a success.

6   Some CBT practitioners have told me privately that they are uncomfortable with the many uncritical stories of CBT success. They acknowledge that 'CBT isn't for everyone', and that clients with an experience of recent bereavement, for example, or sexual abuse histories, may not be suitable. Indeed I know of some stories from IAPT services where clients have complained they haven't been helped by CBT but then see counsellors who work much more flexibly and successfully with them.

7   There are reasons to think that some newcomers to CBT may be impressed by its apparently methodical, pseudoscientific nature, but that people with some familiarity with therapy and some critical thinking ability of their own may be less impressed. Also, those with richer emotional lives, and some significant cultural differences, may not work well with CBT, which can be perceived as somewhat mechanical and simplistic.

8   It is acknowledged by the British Association for Behavioural and Cognitive Psychotherapies (BABCP) that CBT trainees are not required to engage in personal development work such as personal therapy or personal development groups. While there is no hard evidence that such work adds to therapist effectiveness, this must raise the suspicion that the subtleties of personal awareness and interpersonal sensitivity may not be as well developed in CBT practitioners as in other practitioners. That CBT can be delivered online also underlines this perception.

9   Given the sheer volume of research that has confirmed the overwhelming importance of the therapeutic relationship itself (regardless of theoretical orientation), and certainly its greater significance for good outcomes than techniques, it must seem strange that a heavily technical approach like CBT (not reliant on relational subtlety, as shown above) has quite recently claimed overwhelming research evidence for itself.

10   In a society that values speed, efficiency and the technical-rational approach, it is no accident that CBT ('conveyor belt therapy') is so highly valued by government health departments, nor that Richard Layard has linked CBT with addressing unemployment. Needless to say, not all of us are happy with this vision of society and its dehumanizing trends.

Let me repeat that CBT has its place. Indeed it might well have an equal place in a revised, truly integrative training. But its elevation to perceived superiority and its uncritical elevation by the UK government obviously invite serious critique. Most even-handed observers respect CBT's merits but simply want the merits of other approaches to be equally respected. (Note, not all observers are even-handed; many despise CBT for its perceived superficiality.) We are told this rebalancing of merits will happen when other approaches produce research of the right calibre. In the meantime, however, many expect that the serious limitations of CBT, as outlined above, will become all too apparent in the years to come. Perhaps this merely mirrors the tendency towards therapeutic fashions from one decade or so to the next.

Further reading

House, R. & Loewenthal, D. (eds) (2008) *Against and For CBT: Towards A Constructive Dialogue?* Ross-on-Wye: PCCS.

Theories of Counselling Practice:

Challenge

Imagine yourself into the mind of anyone who develops his or her own ideas on counselling theory, particularly around critiques of pre-existing approaches, and generate your own views on what drives founders to create new approaches. Weigh up what you think are the uses of counselling theories and what may be unhelpful or redundant. Are there any legitimate limits to what can and cannot be critiqued among the various competing approaches? Consider who opposes such critiques and on what grounds. Is the author being fair to different approaches or is he betraying some unwitting biases? Consider what prevents you from developing and testing out theories of your own. Is there any tacit criterion for deciding who has the right to command respect for his or her theories? Given the continuing abundance of theories in this subject, is it realistic to wait for controlled trials to compare and evaluate them all?

Case Study

Gina, Carole and Linda feel stimulated by the challenge that anyone might create their own articulated theoretical approach to counselling, and they are particularly motivated to promote a feminist component. At first they don't take themselves seriously (they are not American, male, or psychologists), but gradually they become committed to building a theoretical model that does justice to their shared way of working. This is an approach that integrates rigorous assessment with in-depth relational, emotional and existential challenge and coaching. How likely is it that they can succeed in launching a new model? What would they need to do? What might the obstacles be? Is there any reason they should not proceed with this idea? (See Robb, 2007.)

Critical thinking perspectives

Models of therapy appear mostly to arise from the clinical observations and creative theoretical work of certain practitioner-thinkers working in isolation or in small teams. These figures are tacitly assumed to be in a genius-founder category and, barring developments over decades, most trainees seem content to be followers or consumers of these models rather than radical originators themselves. But why should Gina, Carole and Linda not take themselves seriously as critico-creative thinkers (in opposition to acquiescent patriarchal intellectual traditions) and put together their own new approach? Perhaps we should think beyond quasi-timeless ageographical models and begin to create provisional models informed by local knowledge and serving local cultures.

Professional Issues and Infrastructures

Who Owns Counselling?

This may seem an absurd question but it hopefully provokes a number of interesting questions. On the one hand, how can anyone own counselling, any more than anyone can own history, shopping or love? But on the other hand, counselling found in the titles of university courses, professional bodies and books looks like it has a proprietor. The term only began to be used in its current form in the early twentieth century, was promoted by Rogers in the 1940s and in the UK from the 1970s. It's rather a strange word, suggesting advice-giving but strenuously avoiding exactly that activity, and overlapping with psychotherapy so much that people must wonder why the term 'counselling' was ever needed. A large part of the explanation is to do with turf battles between professionals but also about ideologies. The current state of play in the UK is that anyone can use the title of counsellor or psychotherapist but these may very soon become protected in law. However, no-one can prevent the use of the term 'counselling' in everyday life. To say 'He counselled her' cannot be forbidden (even if he isn't a qualified counsellor)! Interestingly, if we say 'He gave her psychotherapy', this has a different flavour; it may at first suggest charlatanism (if he wasn't qualified) but on closer linguistic analysis we may see that terminology disguises a great deal of uncertainty.

Counselling at its simplest is about two people sitting down in privacy and one of them listening intently and responding helpfully to the other expressing his or her concern about problems in living. No-one can own this. However, specific therapeutic models may be owned, or legally protected, especially in the USA. Primal therapy, for example, was legally protected, or trademarked, as was EMDR (eye movement desensitization and reprocessing). To what extent this is about commercial profit or concern for malpractice is a moot point. Perhaps we can say that 'low key' counselling may be harmless whereas ambitious, defence-attacking and regressive therapies can be dangerous. It's certainly true that human beings often exploit and abuse others, in many settings, and this is probably the strongest justification for enforceable professional ethics, but it's not clear that ownership is the best way of ensuring or maximizing safety.

Legal ownership of a set of therapeutic principles is contentious but probably unstoppable. Pharmaceutical companies are well known for their commercial ownership principles, which maximize their profits but can lead to the immoral withholding of life-saving treatments in certain cases. Obviously professional bodies do not operate in the same way but their procedures do limit the accessibility of training and qualifications, and heavily imply that professional counselling is superior to 'amateur' counselling. This distinction has sometimes become acute in the voluntary sector, where well qualified counsellors may work for no pay but refuse to be perceived as working less professionally. Some groups of American feminist therapists have protested against the corporate ownership of therapy. In the UK, groups like the Independent Practitioners' Network (IPN) have protested against professional bodies' tendencies to 'own' or control therapeutic practice and have sought to find alternative ways of protecting quality.

It looks very much as if there are two quite distinct kinds of ownership problem. The first is commercial exploitation, which many will defend as the right of any creator of new services, products or intellectual properties. The second is ownership by professionalism and this may contain both (some) financial motives (limiting membership, encouraging or causing higher fees or salaries, etc.) and protection of the public motives. The law on patents and ownership is complicated but based on commercial rights. When someone invents or creates a distinctive system of talking therapy, should they not have the right to benefit financially and to control the use of that therapy, or at least the name under which they invented, patented or safeguarded it? The logic of authorship and profit supports this view but can be challenged, as can professional logic, and I turn to such challenges now.

We live in – and as a large social group we have created – a society that accepts capitalism as the economic norm, and this means that profit-seeking and 'wage slavery' are built into our very way of life and work. As well as raw capitalism we have the professions, classically medicine, law, accountancy and so on, which have come to be indispensable. Medicine at least has certain life and death features, whereas many other professions do not: they are supportive of and predatory upon other aspects of social life; they are also bureaucratic. Anarchist and communist critiques of commerce and the professions point to their exploitative nature and their unavoidable linkage with affluence for winners and poverty for losers. Nobody should own anything, say the anarchists; the state should own everything, say the communists. Perhaps none of these three political systems works. Certainly capitalism has many unfortunate side-effects, including poverty, stress, selfishness and legal bureaucracies.

Original counselling was a grassroots movement, linked with voluntary organizations and resistant to medical models of psychological help and intervention. It would not be true to say it was 'owned by the people', rather, the issue of ownership hardly arose. Passion and faith were the engines. Perhaps this was also at odds with psychoanalysis as an elitist, proprietorial venture, somewhere between a craft and a profession. But time has led to professionalization, to professional bodies, accreditation schemes, statutory regulation and to each clinical profession's jealous protection of itself and battle with others. Although it is not usually put in this way, some psychoanalysts seem to believe that 'We have the knowledge and expertise, and we should have the right to ownership of a superior professional reputation'. CBT professionals are also anxious that those perceived to be less well trained in CBT should not be confused with them, hence they will seek ownership via training approved by them.

It's difficult to arrive at a neat answer to the question of who owns counselling. Ultimately it must come down to the challenge that counselling is not about ownership at all. Ownership and professionalization are unfortunately side-shows. Counselling was always only a means of addressing mental health needs, problems in living and individual aspirations to a richer inner life. When counselling becomes part of the problem – part of capitalism's disingenuous structures of professional bureaucracies and commercial enterprises – then it's time to radically re-examine it. We have yet to analyse rigorously the socio-economic sources of, and hence remedies for, human distress.

Further reading

House, R. & Totton, N. (eds) (1997) *Implausible Professions: Arguments for Pluralism.* Ross-on-Wye: PCCS.

Do we Need Supervision Forever?

Under this title I intend to look briefly at a set of questions: (1) What is supervision for? (2) How much supervision do we need? (3) What grounds or evidence do we have for believing in the necessity of supervision? It should be noted at the outset that clinical supervision is mandated by the BACP and some other professional bodies and that one is not actually free to dispense with it. The BACP stipulates that all practitioners must have regular supervision (usually not less than 1.5 hours monthly) and throughout their professional career. Students on accredited courses have a higher ratio expectation.

It is usually claimed that supervision is necessary in order to safeguard clients, to enhance effective practice, to support counsellors and generally to act as a quality control mechanism for the profession. Supervision is a distinguishing characteristic of counselling that is sometimes misunderstood because many other professions make no such similar demand. Psychoanalysts do not face the same requirement. The particular mandatory requirement is also for the most part a UK-specific one. But counselling supervision has been presented positively as a mark of the seriousness of the profession.

However, it is not clear what the precise purposes of supervision are and whether these can be supported by any thoroughgoing rationale or evidence. In principle it sounds good to claim that supervision is there in order to protect clients; it seems logical that if you have to discuss all your clients with a supervisor, then any inappropriate work will be picked up and dealt with. This may in fact happen for trainees with low caseloads but is quite unlikely for busy full-time counsellors with high caseloads. However experienced or perspicacious supervisors may be (and there is no way of determining this), how could any of them definitely know that the supervisee is presenting all her cases or all aspects of them? In other words, supervision cannot guarantee to eliminate or even identify substandard practice or malpractice. It may or may not do so. Generally counsellors are free to choose and change supervisors themselves, as they wish, unless allocated to specific supervisors within organizations. Supervision may *aspire* to protect clients, but that is all.

We can also see that supervision may act as a safety net for supervisees, insofar as they can use it to express any anxieties and distress about their practice and to offload stress and problem solve any issues of stress arising. Counsellors are perhaps always at some risk of secondary trauma. When professional and ethical dilemmas arise, these can be dealt with in a timely fashion, supported by an experienced colleague. It can certainly be argued that one of the peculiar stresses of counselling is its confidentiality, which is made easier by access to a supervisor who shares in the confidentiality. But sometimes, despite all this, counsellors will still experience stress and go off sick. Supervision cannot prevent this and indeed supervisors may on occasion recommend sick leave or become sick themselves.

In the matter of supervision as a means of enhancing the effectiveness of practice, I believe it remains true that no evidence is forthcoming to support this claim. It sounds as if it should act in this way (after all, someone is always paying for the supervision) but let's remind ourselves that many North American therapists receive little or no clinical supervision beyond their training period, simply because it has not been an expectation of the professional culture. It seems doubtful whether practitioners working in a supervision-free culture are less effective than UK counsellors. Also, it is extremely difficult to conduct empirical research on this topic because a control group of unsupervised counsellors would be working unethically according to BACP requirements. If we throw group supervision into the equation, it is even possible to argue that counsellors could be so overwhelmed by contradictory feedback as to become less effective!

Consider finally that supervision is mandatory for all counsellors regardless of caseload and experience. Someone in practice for 30 or 40 years must still have supervision, even if it is difficult to find a suitably experienced supervisor. Anecdotal evidence has it that some counsellors have found their supervision more of a ritual than a meaningful form of assistance. The mandatory nature of supervision for all disregards the possibility that some practitioners are intrinsically more creative, intelligent and effective than others. It acts as a blanket of putative reassurance of quality but we have very little evidence either way. We could probably come up with better schemes combining flexible supervision with tailored continuing professional development and personal therapy, as well as self-supervision. But the tradition of largely one-to-one regular supervision we have inherited, with its emphasis on 'the supervisory relationship', arguably substitutes professional mystique for reason and evidence.

Further reading

Crocket, K., Pentecost, M., Cresswell, R., Paice, C., Tollestrup, D., De Vries, M. & Wolfe, R. (2009) Informing supervision practice through research: a narrative enquiry. *Counselling and Psychotherapy Research,* 9 (2), 101–107.

Feltham, C. (2000) Counselling supervision: baselines, problems and possibilities. In B. Lawton & C. Feltham (eds), *Taking Supervision Forward: Enquiries and Trends in Counselling and Psychotherapy.* London: Sage.

Where is Research Taking us?

It has been evident for decades that psychotherapists and counsellors are immersed in *faith* in their work and relatively uninterested in proving its effectiveness to outsiders. Please note the 'relatively'. Psychoanalysts have always promoted case studies, and following on from them many others have produced case study support for counselling. Carl Rogers pioneered the study of audio-recorded counselling. As counselling found its way into academic settings and more recently into health service settings, the demand for research has increased. Since Hans Eysenck (1952) and other psychologists criticized both the relative lack of research evidence and its perceived poor quality, the North American and British psychotherapy and counselling communities have generated a great deal of research to demonstrate that therapy works and to show how it works. As the BACP and other professional bodies have promoted the cause of professionalization and statutory regulation, inevitably they have had to demonstrate that counselling is as robust as other clinical professions.

Inevitably, I think, when proponents of an activity claim that it makes clients feel better and helps them to overcome stubborn personal health problems, they invite investigation. Someone is always paying for counselling and they have a right to know if claims to success are true, for example whether counselling improves on what time itself often achieves (so-called spontaneous remission); whether counselling acts like a placebo (that is, it stirs up a kind of faith that apparently heals but has no actual active ingredients); whether successes are lasting; which therapeutic approaches achieve good outcomes compared with others; whether counselling is cost effective compared with medication; whether clients want and are satisfied with counselling; and so on. Academics and postgraduate trainees have a natural interest in quantifying the success of counselling but also in generating original research questions about the many subtle processes involved in counselling. Hence, we have a burgeoning research movement focusing on both quantitative and qualitative concerns and the methodologies designed to yield relevant data. The BACP now requires a significant research input on all accredited courses.

On the face of it this is no bad thing and it will bring counselling into line with what clinical psychology has claimed it to be for decades – that is, 'scientifically reputable' and evidence-based. There are, however, many problems that are often glossed over and even suppressed. It is not a strong argument but a significant one that many counsellors are probably good at what they do (namely, they relate intimately, subtly and helpfully to other people) precisely because they are not so good at the technical and scientific tasks involved in research, such as systematic measurement. Quite often counselling trainees dislike, avoid and perform poorly on research-oriented requirements. They may be happy to leave research to others better qualified or more suited to it, provided these researchers go about it fairly and sympathetically. But there are good reasons for thinking that the scientist-practitioner model beloved by psychologists isn't necessarily the best model. Even Hans Eysenck conceded that excellent practitioners may not be excellent researchers and vice versa. So who was it that decided, on what grounds, to insist on taking up valuable time in counselling training trying to turn all counsellors into researchers? Research awareness for all may be an important aim but even here it is quite possible that an excellent practitioner may find research difficult, boring and unfruitful. Is there actually any evidence that research-informed counsellors make more effective or safer counsellors than those who ignore or fail to appreciate formal empirical research?

We have seen in the case of CBT the assumption being made that an apparent abundance of irrefutable confirmatory research for one approach creates an impression that other approaches are either ineffective or less effective than CBT. In other words, a relative absence of confirmatory research is incorrectly taken as evidence that something is dubious. Now, it may well be that this implicit challenge generates masses of effectiveness research that will equally support, say, psychodynamic and humanistic forms of therapy. After all, we have had plenty of past research apparently confirming that all therapies are equal. We have had lots of research telling us that it is the therapeutic relationship, not theories and techniques, that determines successful outcomes. How can the latter be true when we are now being told that CBT is overwhelmingly successful, when CBT is one of the least relationship-focused of approaches? How can it be true that, according to some research, untrained helpers, trainees and beginners may often be perceived as being as or more helpful than experienced practitioners? And if it is true, should we take seriously the statement that research is full of surprises, and abandon training altogether? Of course, I am condensing various findings here, and some will say that all such research has to be examined very carefully, and repeated again and again. But the underlying points here are that (a) research findings often contradict each other; (b) we commonly ignore research when its outcomes don't suit us; and (c) we are in no hurry to conduct fundamental research into practices that we hold as sacrosanct (e.g. into how essential supervision and personal development really are).

Much postgraduate research is chosen on the basis of students' personal interests, utilizing small scale qualitative methods and yielding unsurprising and often trivial results. Exactly what do we hope research in counselling will unearth? I heard a counselling researcher passionately defending research by comparing it with medicine – you wouldn't want to be seen by a doctor who was completely out of touch with up-to-date findings. The latter is quite true, in the medical field. But what has counselling research found substantively and what can it be hoped to find? Many counsellors object to the assumption that counselling is a health practice or that it has specific curative goals. Can it ever be compared with cancer research? Are we ever going to discover the equivalent of the genome? The point here is that it is extremely unlikely that we are working in a field that will ever yield dramatic findings. Research will no doubt consolidate the position of counselling, filling in some small gaps in practice knowledge and suggesting small ways in which practice can be adjusted. It may sometimes conclusively validate or disconfirm the claims of certain approaches or techniques. But much of the time it will repeat what is known or remains inconclusive. The danger is that the counselling and psychotherapy professions are uncritically buying into the fetishism of a research and information overload which also dominates other aspects of our lives. In other parts of this book I suggest there may be ways of expanding counselling that are not chained to empirical research.

It is contentious to suggest that many practitioners view research as boring and irrelevant, and the observation that much of it is trivial is also controversial. But the onus is on the research community to demonstrate convincingly that theirs is not simply a public relations exercise in advancing the profession and their own livelihoods.

Further reading

Cooper, M. (2008) *Essential Research Findings in Psychotherapy and Counselling: The Facts Are Friendly*. London: Sage.

Feltham, C. (2004) Evidence-based counselling and psychotherapy in the UK: critique and alternatives. *Journal of Contemporary Psychotherapy,* 35 (1), 131–144.

Kline, P. (1992) Problems of methodology in studies of psychotherapy. In W. Dryden & C. Feltham (eds), *Psychotherapy and its Discontents*. Buckingham: Open University Press.

Is Statutory Regulation a Good and Inevitable Development?

Counselling and psychotherapy have been lumbering towards some sort of regulation for many decades, all the while being reasonably well regulated voluntarily by their own professional bodies. Superficially the movement towards a professionalized status may be seen as natural and inevitable, insofar as many similar movements such as nursing seem to follow the same path: a needed and good thing starts as a grass-roots, voluntary activity and becomes in time a university-affiliated, state-regulated enterprise. Thereby, standards are guaranteed, quality is improved, practitioners are account-able, charlatans and malpractice are weeded out, an evidence base is uti-lized, the public are protected, employment is boosted, and so on. That is the standard claim and logic of the growth of the professions. On the face of it, such a presentation is hard to refute: why would we *not* want to endorse all that? And of course it is the route recommended by the professional bodies.

The Health Professions Council (HPC) is currently taking this develop-ment forward, with close links with the Department of Health. Counselling and psychotherapy are being regarded as health professions, an identity which many reject. There is some danger that the HPC, with no accurate grasp of this field, would distort it and overshadow its professional bodies. Practition-ers would be restricted to a certain title and might see their practice affected in various undesirable ways. Membership costs would rise and clients would be affected.

Opposition to state regulation has its origins in the nature of psychoanaly-sis and humanistic therapies. The focus is the individual client in all his or her precious uniqueness. The focus is not upon the standardized goals of health care or social adaptation. The client sets the agenda, which may proceed as deeply and lengthily as necessary. The course of each therapy is unpredict-able and things may get worse before they get better. The client may discover the unexpected, may remember things previously forgotten, may make radical lifestyle changes, may become either more or less 'productive' in the eyes of others. The practitioner is trustworthy and self-regulatingly 'professional', has invested in his or her own training, often works from home, is creative and may take therapeutic risks, may work on a relatively low income, may have politi-cally left-leaning views. Essentially both approaches have some ingredients that are implicitly critical of society. Psychoanalysis was certainly regarded as radical in its own original time and place, and the humanistic therapies stem-ming from the 1960s were also very radical. Probably most such opposition comes from private practitioners who arguably have least to gain from state regulation and most to lose. Many independent practitioners may have cho-sen their vocation in preference to anything too closely associated with state bureaucracies.

As I was writing this (mid-2009) I received news from the BACP that the HPC is moving towards a protection of title, standards of proficiency and levels of entry to a statutory register. These may distinguish sharply between counsellor and psychotherapist, with the former being pegged at level 5 and the latter at level 7. The implications would include the claim that psychotherapists were more capable of addressing severe mental disorders and more diagnostically knowledgeable. Counsellors would be linked with wellbeing and obstacles to wellbeing, and to 'life problems, issues and transitions'. Anyone who knows the worlds of counselling and psychotherapy from the inside knows how absurd these pseudo-distinctions are. Even the far from radical BACP altogether rejects the distinction between counselling and psychotherapy made by the HPC. But if things move in this direction, there will be implications. As an associated illustration, in the world of accountancy there are accountants proper and accounting technicians, and much (though not all) of what they do is identical. But of course accountants earn more even when doing the same work, or when getting accounting technicians to do such work while they invoice their clients for much more than they pay those accounting technicians who they subcontract the work to. Similar absurdities and exploitative manoeuvres can be seen across clinical and counselling psychology, and psychiatry.

Documentation on statutory regulation contains layers of misunderstanding, prejudice and absurd distinctions that would fit in well with the Swiftian world of *Gulliver's Travels*. At root it probably has little to do with its declared aims and everything to do with tradition, prejudice, snobbery, public relations and vested interests. Such is (part of) the world we live in, and that we seem to have little power to change. Perhaps only a shift towards common sense or anarchism could change it.

Further reading

Mace, C., Rowland, N., Evan, C., Schroder, T. & Halstead, J. (2009) Psychotherapy professionals in the UK: expansion and experiment. *European Journal of Psychotherapy and Counselling,* 11 (2), 131–140.

Postle, D. (2007) *Regulating the Psychological Therapies: From Taxonomy to Taxidermy.* Ross-on-Wye: PCCS Books.

What are the Differences between Counselling, Psychotherapy, Psychoanalysis, Clinical and Counselling Psychology?

We might add to this list psychiatry, mental health nursing and coaching. The gist of this question is that we have a number of mental health professions and emerging professions that have many overlaps in what they do. (I have avoided here going into the caveat that some practitioners would disown the soubriquet of mental health professional in favour of personal growth facilitator or psycho-practitioner.) The easy response to the question is along the lines of the following: each of these professional identities is determined by its history and key figures, each of them intersects with others and each has something distinct to offer its target client group. A middle position on the question might be that there are distinct activities belonging to each group but also overlaps, that this can lead to some confusion but that paying careful attention to claims and identities will hopefully clarify everything. A final, highly critical view is this: all such groups, claiming or aspiring to be professions, essentially address the same problems of mental distress and all are engaged in turf wars to protect their territory, and thereby wasting resource and doing a disservice to clients. The first we might call an example of conservative thinking, the second of cautious thinking and the third of radical critical thinking.

It is indeed true that these professions all stem from slightly different historical periods and each is housed under a different organizational roof. It is not true that they co-exist peacefully and without rancour. However, it is possible for a single individual to be simultaneously a member of two or more of these groups. A psychoanalyst may work partly as a psychoanalytic psycho-therapist, a clinical psychologist as a psychotherapist, a psychotherapist as a counsellor, and so on. This may be due to a wish for varied work or to meet a range of clients, or a need to spread your bets pragmatically in a competitive job market; in other words, it may be due to ideological leanings or to self-protective economic calculations.

Put simply (and I apologize if this is too simple or a borderline caricature), psychoanalysts train for longer, have extensive analysis of their own and usually treat patients in private practice several times a week for several years. (Note that the terms 'patient' and 'client' are part of this distinguishing between the professions.) Psychotherapists, who usually train for three to five years, were traditionally mainly psychoanalytic in orientation but are now spread across the humanistic and CBT approaches; they see patients/clients in private practice or other settings once, twice or three times a week, often for months or years; their patients/clients might have severe and deeply-rooted problems.

Clinical psychologists have psychology degrees up to doctoral level, are very research aware, probably have some training in two or more approaches, work mostly salaried within the NHS but in other settings too and may specialize in certain severe client problems. Counselling psychologists are relatively new and many of them are also simply counsellors but with a psychology degree and BPS status. Psychiatrists are medically qualified and have high caseloads, often act-ing as managers rather than closely hands-on clinicians; they engage in formal psychodiagnosis, have statutory powers and prescribe medication and other treatments, and may or may not engage in in-depth talking therapy. Mental health nurses (previously psychiatric nurses) work in hospitals and in the com-munity, seeing patients for certain disorders but sometimes doing counselling.

Historically counsellors arrived in the 1970s, using mainly psychodynamic and humanistic principles with a wide range of clients; their training usually lasts from two to four years; and they work in a variety of settings. Coach-ing (also mentoring) is a relatively new activity directed at helping employees, children, sportspeople and others to improve their functioning; a great deal of counselling theory overlaps with counselling and psychotherapy theory.

Each of the above professional groups has its unique history and profes-sional organization (e.g. British Psychoanalytic Council, United Kingdom Council for Psychotherapy, British Psychological Society, Royal College of Psychiatrists, British Association for Counselling and Psychotherapy; and there are others). Training traditions vary and curricula differ somewhat too. Often when battles arise it will be said that one training is much longer and more rigorous than others. It is claimed that client groups differ in the depth and complexity of distress or disorder, and that therapy or treatment varies enormously in skill, precision and effectiveness. Psychiatrists are paid most and have the highest status, then come clinical psychologists, then (probably) psychotherapists, with unclear comparative incomes among mental health nurses and counsellors. Clearly there is a pecking order.

The biggest perennial 'battle' concerns the relative merits and identities of counselling and psychotherapy. Some sincerely argue that there are distinct differences, while others (including the BACP and the person-centred community) assert that there are no real differences. Battle lines are crudely drawn. Alleged differences can be exaggerated and distorted. At stake are sincere beliefs, identities and livelihoods, but also prejudices and snobbery. The confidential and idiosyncratic nature of therapeutic practice (as well as diagnostic imprecision) means that we usually cannot know what actually goes on within sessions and so cannot accurately compare. It seems likely that the best practitioners – those who genuinely put the client first – work flexibly and unpretentiously, probably willing to refer clients on to alternative practitioners when it is in the client's interests.

The key problems of the competing clinical professions are these. There are serious socio-economic injustices regarding status and income. There are serious inefficiencies involved – that is, wastage in terms of duplicated services and layers of confusion regarding assessment and referral. It is confusing for ordinary people struggling to find the most suitable help for themselves and their loved ones, not only in terms of who to see but also regarding how much one should expect to pay. All these problems probably stem ultimately from historical inertia, misunderstanding and a resistance to change, perhaps partly from self-protective dishonesty, but overwhelmingly from traditions of belief, practice and bureaucracy that make change inordinately difficult. I do not personally accept a conservative or cautious middle position on this question.

Further reading

Cheshire, K. & Pilgrim, D. (2004) *A Short Introduction to Clinical Psychology.* London: Sage.

Gask, L. (2004) *A Short Introduction to Psychiatry.* London: Sage.

Milton, J., Polmear, C. & Fabricius, J. (2004) *A Short Introduction to Psychoanalysis.* London: Sage.

31

How Buoyant or Otherwise is
the Job Market
for Counsellors?

I completed my initial training in 1981 and spent several years after that working in a probation hostel where I did some counselling but was not primarily a counsellor. This was due purely to a paucity of employment opportunities for counsellors, even in London. Years later, in the 1990s in Sheffield, I moved from self-employment into academia, partly due to the unreliability of an income in private counselling and training when I had a family to support. Along the way I have seen examples of a few entrepreneurial counsellors making very good money but many others struggling to get any paid foothold within counselling. I have been most acutely aware of this latter trend as a university tutor, watching students graduate and struggle to find paid work. This is an open secret. But I don't think it has ever been fully and openly, ethically addressed by the professional bodies or universities and colleges. It is not in the interests of those who profit from the talking therapies to address it. Interestingly, I had it put to me that a topic like this doesn't really belong in a book on critical thinking, the implication being that critical thinking is for serious intellectual matters and counsellor employment does not qualify as such. I disagree sharply, considering that radical honesty and truth-seeking demand attention be given to such socio-economically critical issues.

One line taken is that counselling is a 'portfolio career' in which you may have a small private practice, a part-time job in counselling or a related field, and some work in your original profession. Some trained counsellors are content and able to do voluntary (unpaid) counselling, often because they have supportive working partners or have taken early retirement. Many counselling jobs are part-time (perhaps half-time) or sessional, such as a number of half days or so many hours a week. Usually counselling is modestly paid. Some people do not change their job but absorb counselling skills into their job in some way. To my knowledge, most interviewees for counselling courses will be made aware of this state of affairs but will still want to go ahead.

The kind of scenario I find particularly troubling is as follows. A woman, a single parent in her early 50s, pays for counselling training on her credit card. She has a background in mental health work, she is an able student and counsellor. But she cannot find paid work as a counsellor. The reasons are: (1) above all, there are very few jobs in the region; (2) of the very few jobs available and for which she gets an interview, hundreds of others have applied, many of them less well qualified and some better qualified; (3) there is a gap in her CV for those years in which she was raising her children; and (4) paradoxically, because she is so desperate to get the job, she becomes over-anxious at interview. Anyway, the result is that she doesn't get jobs and this dents her self-esteem and hope. And while she keeps looking for work there is still very little and she simply gets older and less confident. I have also known competent younger people fail to get counselling work. Generally, after a few years of trying, they give up and drift into something else. Occasionally people in this position will take yet another (higher or specialized) course (and gamble) in the hope of strengthening their CV.

Obviously, some do find paid counselling work, but this is usually part-time. There is the conundrum that you can't get a job until you have strong relevant experience, and you cannot get that until you have a job. There is also the catch that you cannot get a job until you are accredited, and you cannot get accredited without first spending a few years in a voluntary capacity accumulating sufficient hours to apply for accreditation (the world of Catch-22). Also, you're more likely to get a job if you're mobile, that is, able to move to any part of the country, which for people with complex parental or family responsibilities and roots may be a non-starter. As if all this were not depressing enough, it isn't unusual to hear comments passed about people who *did* get a good counselling job (as if there must be something wrong with you if you didn't) or asides about attitude, not trying hard enough and so on – 'blame the loser'.

Little strong, accurate information is available on job prospects for counsellors. Anecdotally, it seems that areas like London obviously have the most openings (but also the most courses and applicants) and the NHS probably is the strongest hope, but often prefers people with previous NHS experience and increasingly prefers its own training routes for IAPT work. Some services will do very little, if any, open advertising, and instead will circulate fliers and emails which may or may not reach everyone they should. Often, people who are internal to organizations stand the best chance of getting an advertised job, in spite of equal opportunities policies; perhaps because they know the set-up, they know what to say and ask. There is plenty of help available for improving your CV, practising your interview skills and so on, but at the end of the day in a highly competitive economy there are only so many jobs to go around, and the counselling market isn't well funded.

Statutory services like clinical psychology will know how many practitioners are needed in any area and fund training accordingly. There is no way of being certain about how many counsellors and psychotherapists are needed and the extent of private practice is unknown. But in principle it should be relatively easy for the professional bodies to log counselling agencies in all areas, including numbers of full- and part-time staff, turnover, pay, specialisms, etc. Something similar might be done for voluntary agencies and private practice. It would need regular updating and might prove too complicated but it could provide a valuable picture and might help to suggest how many counsellors are needed and therefore the extent of any training needed. Unfortunately it is very likely that if this happened it would confirm what already seems obvious on the ground – that too many training courses are turning out too many counsellors. This is profitable for colleges, universities and other training institutes, as well as for professional bodies and associated industries (supervision, insurance, publishing, conference and training venues, etc.). It also holds out hope to people who seek meaningful work like counselling. But I suspect there is something dishonest involved in it all. In the meantime a warning should be given to all course applicants that counselling is a vocation resembling art, drama and writing – highly desired but with relatively few concrete openings – and many trained counsellors are like out-of-work actors.

Further reading

Feltham, C. (1993) Making a living as a counsellor. In W. Dryden (ed.), *Questions and Answers for Counselling in Action*. London: Sage.

32

How should we Respond to Clients' Views and Complaints?

I want to discuss here the kinds of views or feedback given by clients and ex-clients verbally or via evaluation mechanisms, research or their own publications. On the positive side, clients have often said, unsurprisingly, that they benefit from being listened to, from warmth, acceptance and understanding and that they prefer talking therapies to medication. A majority (let's say 80 per cent) appear to benefit overall from counselling. In the 'middle range' some clients have called for better explanations of what counselling is and does and for more guidance and advice than most counsellors give. At the frankly negative end, some have complained about (some) counsellors being too detached, sometimes abusive or uninterested in their views and too insistent on their (the counsellors') own interpretations. Clients have obviously complained when agreements or norms have been broken (e.g. regarding confidentiality and sexual contact) but have also complained about counselling taking too long with no discernible improvements, and practitioners being too rigid in their personal manner and way of working. Anecdotally, I have also heard occasional stories about counselling sessions being intruded upon in certain service settings, clients being unhappy about questionnaires, wanting a different counsellor or a better match, needing childcare or flexible appointments.

These are the things we do hear about and we must assume (indeed we know) that many clients are wary of complaining. Reluctance to complain is probably complicated. Many clients by the nature of their personal problems are probably quite unassertive and passive. Many will regard the counsellor as an authority figure, perhaps akin to a GP, and may assume that if they are not feeling any better it is their fault, they're not trying hard enough or they're beyond help. Many will realize that there is little choice, that the counselling service has very few counsellors anyway. In some cases there may be a poor fit between counsellor and client or an experience of getting off on the wrong foot. As in any profession, a few counsellors probably will deliver a less than optimal service or will inadvertently or consciously exploit or abuse the client. Lest we are tempted to resort to the 'bad apples' line of reasoning, we should remember that most of us are susceptible to errors, inattention and occasional personality clashes.

Clients may be in a one-down position on two or three fronts. First, they will usually have a problem which preoccupies them and makes them doubt themselves and can lead to struggle with everyday challenges. Second, for the most part they do not know any theories of counselling or its terminology; counsellors have often had therapy themselves, have read widely and also seen many clients. The asocial nature of counselling – its asymmetrical style, lack of small talk, silences, expectation of honesty and seriousness and its barely comprehended transferential features – means that the client is in alien territory. He or she has to figure out the tacit rules, then weigh up the counsellor and the prospects that this is going to be helpful, or not. Sometimes the client will be aware that time is precious, either being paid for or being quite limited. A great deal is going on mentally for the client. Third, the client has to gauge both how much she can trust the counsellor, and how far she can relax her defences, confront pain and risk, and make the effort to change.

In principle, counsellors will anticipate all such problems at the initial stages; they will facilitate and remain open to feedback throughout the therapeutic process, use supervision wisely and try to resolve any problems directly with their clients. Clients who are dissatisfied can complain to the professional bodies. It has often been suggested that counsellors should explain their practice clearly at the outset but we cannot know if this happens and it is, anyway, difficult to explain transferential dynamics. It has also been suggested that all counsellors should provide an information sheet with professional body details and guidance on the typical course of counselling and its ethics. Such measures should forestall some problems and client complaints.

Much more difficult are the following. Since long-term therapy in private practice entails high expense and incurs quite a few complaints, long-term practitioners need to be very clear about their rationale for it and they should often review progress. Clients should be advised (perhaps by the kind of information sheet advocated above) that there are many models and ways of working, and certain choices, for example between short-term and long-term therapies. Supervisors need to be alert to how many clients their supervisees are carrying at any one time; they need to have some knowledge of each client and some awareness that all practitioners will have blind spots and bad days. And supervisors should consider that it is conceivable that they have at least one supervisee who is too rigid, who sometimes knowingly or subtly abuses a client or offers a substandard service.

Much more difficult to get at is an awareness on the part of any counsellor that her interpersonal style may be jarring for some clients, or her theoretical orientation inappropriate for some. Some clients will clearly want a quite con-crete kind of help and will not locate the source of their distress in their past, while others will not find it helpful to be required to fill in questionnaires or undertake homework. For almost all counsellors, the idea of offering clients advice and guidance is unwelcome and counter to most professional norms, yet some flexibility or better explanation of norms might help somewhat. The 'human touch' should never be far away.

Let's not forget that a proportion of clients may misperceive or under-value what has been happening in counselling, or may not have put much effort into it, and that a minority are litigious. This is not about blaming clients but about being realistic. The customer is not always right but should always be taken seriously and always be dealt with professionally. But 'professional' should never come to mean distant, inflexible and unresponsive.

Further reading

Bates, Y. (2006) *Shouldn't I Be Feeling Better by Now? Client Views of Therapy.* Basingstoke: Palgrave.

Sands, A. (2000) *Falling for Therapy: Psychotherapy from Clients' Point of View.* Basingstoke: Palgrave.

Professional Issues and Infrastructures:

Professional bodies' policies and pronunciations, and the weight of the history of counselling generally, may seem daunting for individual beginners and practitioners

to take on critically. But established thought systems can become stale, complacent and out of touch, and need critical input if they are to remain relevant and honest. Counsellors encourage clients to be open and honest and there is good reason to believe that these values should carry over into the profession itself. What vested interests might shore up counselling traditions and prevent significant critical scrutiny? The ingredients of all professions tend to become somewhat carved in stone and difficult to shift after some years. Who determines the usefulness of supervision or perhaps even the usefulness of research itself? Is counselling at a point where, for public relations reasons, it must appear solid and coherent, and deny its flaws and inconsistencies? Must it be consistent? Think of alternative ways of construing this activity of helping people that we call counselling.

Karen has recently completed counselling training and has a psychology degree. She is torn between pursuing a route towards counselling psychologist status and a career in the NHS, and other possibilities. She has some sympathies with radical humanistic approaches, with the Independent Practitioners' Network, and the prospects for private practice. What are the pros and cons of each course of action practically, financially and ideologically? To what extent does this scenario resonate with any questions facing you? (See House, 2003; Orlans & Van Scoyoc, 2009.)

Critical thinking perspectives

We might characterize Karen's first choice as a 'straight' one with fewer risks and higher potential financial benefits, with the second and more radical choice representing greater idealism and higher risks. Some are probably attracted to statutory professions because they mesh with their personalities and beliefs in tradition and 'correctness'; conversely, others will mistrust the establishment and seek marginal or oppositional positions. And of course the very wish to become a helping or caring professional has been analysed in terms of seeking a reparative experience. One might think that careers guidance is easy to access, especially for those already within a counselling environment, but this isn't necessarily true. Karen might pragmatically pursue the counselling psychology path, giving herself the later possibility of having a foot in both (NHS and private practice) camps. Radical critics of the standard analysis of mental health and mental health professions might well argue these are incorrigibly flawed and we are in need of revolutionary changes.

Counselling, Society and Culture

How Important are 'Social Contexts of Counselling' as a Component of Training?

It has been understood, indeed demanded, that counselling training courses include material on the social contexts of counselling. This suggests a corrective to the otherwise overly individual focus of the counselling curriculum. Each of us does not live in a vacuum: social relationships form us, impinge on us and help us to recover. Social institutions (education, work, religion, culture, healthcare) contain, form and sometimes oppress us. We do not live in a monolithic society as passive social cogs but usually in families within subgroups in a multicultural society, as unique individuals. Society contains many neglected and caricatured minority groups, members of which may suffer disproportionately from identity problems. The culture of counselling itself is often criticized for being too white, heterosexual, middle class and female. A profession that sets such store by principles of fairness and respect must logically open itself up to examination.

Quite often social contexts have been interpreted in so-called 'politically correct' terms to refer to oppressed and minority groups: women; ethnic minority and black people; gay, lesbian, bisexual, transvestite and transgender people; disabled people; working-class people; people from non-majority religious, spiritual and cultural groups; vulnerable young and old people. The terms 'difference' and 'diversity' are sometimes used to refer to these and to the 'mainstream' groups in the UK, and efforts have been made to make white people more conscious of their identity and privileges. It is acknowledged that it is practically impossible for training courses to include detailed material and guidance on all such topics but it is recommended that all counsellors are made aware of pertinent issues of identity, power and discrimination.

The UK population is approaching 62 million. What was a predominantly white, Christian country has become a highly multicultural nation in the last few decades. Assumptions and prejudices about the alleged perversity and rarity of gay people have been overturned by statistics and openness. Disability is seen not only as a fairly common phenomenon but also as something anyone is susceptible to. Unfair treatment of ethnic minorities and recognition of the stresses of oppression and racism have led to some improvements in awareness and the law. However, problems remain. Women are not a minority but a patriarchal tradition stretching back millennia ensures that change is slow, and women still face discrimination. These are regularly aired in the media but need to be exposed in counselling training.

Social contexts, however, refer to more than these issues. While it is sometimes claimed that class is no longer an issue and that we live in a fluid meritocracy, quite clearly there are wide disparities in wealth in what is a 'First World' capitalist country. Whether great wealth comes from hard work and shrewd business endeavours, or from inheritance, the rich and affluent enjoy a better lifestyle, more influence, better health and better opportunities for their children. They can buy the services of the best healthcare specialists, presumably including psychotherapists; they can also buy themselves out of many of the problems facing poorer people, most obviously the grinding misery of debt and poverty. Unfortunately surveys of wellbeing and happiness show that often a great deal of our unhappiness is caused by an awareness of our position in the economic pecking order. If you are stuck in a low status job and on low wages, you have fewer opportunities for autonomy and stimulation. While in principle you can engage in 'lifelong learning' and 'better yourself', in reality many are stuck in such lowly positions, and it seems an insult to suggest that the unemployed can use CBT to learn a stoical attitude to the suffering that often comes with their socially lowly position. In any capitalist society there are winners and losers.

Counsellors should, I think, ask themselves where they sit on the socio-economic ladder and what this means about their own attitudes and relationships with clients. If you come from a confident, affluent middle-class home, you are more likely to feel resourceful, to be articulate and hopeful, than those who don't. (There are exceptions, of course.) The very vocabulary we use is highly relevant, and subtle differences between the client's and counsellor's language will transmit themselves. It is infinitely more likely that the counsellor will be a middle-class person and (in private practice) will sit in a smart middle-class house in a middle-class neighbourhood than that the counsellor will be a working-class person counselling from a poor house in a run-down council estate. Class, financial status and their accoutrements command respect in a way that a sheer talent for counselling does not. Counselling in private practice reflects the hierarchical philanthropic tradition of the UK. Even in the voluntary sector, it is quite likely that middle-class women will be counselling clients who are there because they cannot afford to pay for counselling themselves.

These are not minor, niggling matters, but central. Crucially, counselling psychologizes personal problems in living; it encourages individuals to consider what they can do to improve their lot. One writer has referred to the 'hyperindividualism, which in turn is traceable to our radical Protestant heritage and its secular offshoots' (Kirschner, 1996: 60). Unintentionally (but structurally) counsellors distract people from political analysis and action (Cushman, 1996). Obviously not all problems are caused by capitalism but a competitive economic environment hardly prioritizes welfare and altruism. It seems likely that people will get depressed and anxious, that bereavements and divorces will bring heartache, within any political system. The depression that comes with chronic unemployment or unsatisfying, low paid employment might be lessened within a kinder society, however. The loneliness that comes with the sense that each of us bears a peculiar suffering, that we are in some ways inadequate and a burden, might be mitigated by wholly different educational norms focusing on human welfare rather than competitiveness.

It may be that counselling has become necessary – and also thrives – in the current socio-economic conditions. There have certainly been many discussions about making better links in counselling training about the socio-economic causes of mental ill health; and the BACP's declared vision has been encapsulated in the phrase 'Towards an emotionally healthy society'. But unless we are prepared to discuss possible relationships between individual problems in living and the taken-for-granted isolation and competition in which we often live in this kind of capitalist society, we may be fooling ourselves.

Further reading

Pilgrim, D. (1997) *Psychotherapy and Society*. London: Sage.
Proctor, G., Cooper, M., Sanders, P. & Malcolm, B. (eds) (2006) *Politicizing the Person-Centred Approach: An Agenda for Social Change*. Ross-on-Wye: PCCS.
Smail, D. (2005) *Power, Interest and Psychology: Elements of a Social Materialist Understanding of Distress*. Ross-on-Wye: PCCS.

Can Counselling be a
Countercultural Activity?

'Countercultural' is usually taken to mean that which goes against the broad norms of society. The hippie movement of the 1960s was said to be countercultural, and the term is better understood as fairly strongly opposed to prevalent social values and conventions. Postmodernists might well argue that there is no monolithic society against which anyone can be countercultural – rather, there are many trends at any one time. While there is some truth in this, I shall argue that British, and Western, society today is characterized by consumerism, acquiescence in capitalist norms, expectations of continuing economic growth, global competitiveness; by technical, rational and bureaucratic assumptions and procedures; and by accompanying dehumanizing and planet-degrading phenomena – anthropogenic climate change, fossil fuel depletion, a loss of biodiversity, an untenable population increase and international and intercultural tensions. Put more simply, at a certain level we are greedy, self-interested, self-deceived and deceiving of others, ecologically indifferent, intolerant of differences, over-cognitive and under-emotional and patriarchally determined.

Counselling wasn't set up as a political movement but we must consider some of its underpinning values. Generically it is not about directing anyone but about helping its clients to discover and act on their own resources, to be self-determining. It encourages honesty and integrity. It is dedicated to enhancing mental health, part of which is the honouring of the whole human being – including the emotional, physical and spiritual. It helps to distinguish between a real self with basic needs and a false self with inflated wants. Counselling contains a large dose of egalitarianism in its theoretical make-up, and a recognition of the damage done to human beings by overly authoritarian systems and individuals. It recognizes that each individual has unique characteristics and needs.

Contrast all this with societal tendencies towards acquisitiveness, competition, consumerism, knuckling down and so on. Think of woman-oriented birth practices versus technological births; small-scale, child-centred schooling versus mass compulsory education; and meaningful creative work versus soul-destroying jobs. Recall that Freud's original psychoanalysis started to expose the patriarchal norms of nineteenth-century Vienna, including child abuse, the oppression of women, and sexual inhibition. Recall the links between the humanistic therapies that emerged from the 1960s (Gestalt, psychodrama, person-centred, transactional analysis, encounter, primal, etc.) and a climate of student revolt, free love, 'make love not war', the women's movement, anti-racism, communes, mind-expanding drugs, 'back to nature'. You may not espouse all such causes and experiments but we cannot overlook a difference in values here. The human potential movement was not, and is not, about greed and consumerism. Whatever its (fairly obvious) flaws, it contains a certain vision for human beings. That is not the vision being lived by most people today.

In a typical counselling session a client may express frustration with the pressures of his job (if he has one), he may express exasperation at the poor fit between his own talents and aspirations and the actual opportunities available to him. He may protest that the degree he worked hard for has led him nowhere and has incurred a large debt. He may be exasperated by the pressures on him to own and run a car and possess all the technological paraphernalia that characterize our society. He may appreciate the honesty possible in the counselling situation but laugh at the very idea of meaningful, thorough-going honesty with his partner and his boss. He may cry deeply at memories of his own past suffering and the everyday suffering he sees around him but acknowledge that crying is taboo in everyday settings.

On the other hand, if counselling were countercultural, if its values and implications were to be lived out in the world beyond the counselling room, where might it all lead? We are bombarded with disingenuous rhetoric about emotional intelligence, choice, self-fulfilment, lifelong learning, mental health enhancement, gross national happiness, positive psychology, human rights and the like, as if the government were seriously concerned about these and able to deliver them. As we know, politicians are more usually self-serving and focused on short-term economics. Some clients in counselling may feel transiently liberated and determined to change their lives radically so as not to reinforce unhealthy behaviours. Some downshift, become self-employed, more self-sufficient, more community-oriented. In a small way, that is somewhat countercultural.

It's worth a passing thought that the values of autonomy or self-determination in counselling (the right to decide on one's own values and lifestyle), along with anti-authoritarianism, lean towards a philosophy of anarchism. Right-wing libertarians *might* claim such values as their own, and socialists might argue that only a socialist society can deliver the goods. But true anarchy is centrally about self-determination, and is obviously countercultural. However, today's counselling movement has drifted from its original, radically humanistic values, and seeks professional status. It wants to make a contribution to society as it is: counselling in schools, expanded counselling services in the NHS, and so on. There is little sign of truly barefoot psychoanalysts living alternative lifestyles and inspiring others to do likewise. Private practice remains associated with affluent middle-class neighbourhoods and lifestyles.

Further reading

Feltham, C. (2009) Revolutionary claims and visions in psychotherapy: an anthropathological perspective. *Journal of Contemporary Psychotherapy*, 39 (1), 41–53.
Reich, W. (1970) *The Mass Psychology of Fascism*. New York: Noonday.

35

How Much should Counsellors Charge?

It's perfectly possible to work as a counsellor and never have to ask this question. But even the salaried counsellor needs some idea of what their work is worth. At the time of writing, full-time jobs are scarce but salaries typically range between about £20K and £40K per annum depending on the setting –

voluntary sector, NHS, colleges and universities and businesses. A few earn more, and some work voluntarily. Counselling is often considered one of the caring professions, alongside nursing, social work and similar professions, but pays less than clinical psychology and far less than psychiatry.

Counselling – related to psychotherapy and psychoanalysis – has a tradition of freelance or private practice in the UK going back to the 1950s. All that is required is a quiet, private room where two people can sit and talk undisturbed. Very few overheads are involved, unless the counsellor rents a room or office for this purpose. Some think it is more professional to work away from home, perhaps in a dedicated centre with a receptionist, but this might cost an additional 30 per cent approximately, which will be passed on to clients. In reality most counsellors will charge the local going rate, which varies geographically and according to professional hierarchy in the UK from about £30 to £120 an hour. The amount is usually hourly (or per 50 minutes). If we take an average lower figure of £40 an hour and imagine a client attending weekly for six months, that's about £1,000. Paying that amount is probably well worth it if their distress is significantly reduced and the alternative is languishing on a waiting list. So we may argue that this (or more) is a fair price for a desired service.

'I paid an affordable sum and got what I needed', would be a good client testimonial. But counselling is usually a nonlinear and somewhat unpredictable process. It may take a long time, it may prove painful and perhaps for a minority of clients it will produce no improvement, or even a deterioration. The client pays for time and expertise (training, qualifications and length of experience) rather than a palpable product. Compare this with a divorce lawyer who charges, say, £180 an hour for a case whose eventual complexity brings the sum to £10,000 or much more; or a plumber who quotes you a firm price in advance for installing a new heating system and finishes the work at the promised price of £5,000. One involves expert knowledge, intangible processes and unforeseeable elements (as well as office premises, staff, etc.) and the other skilled labour (and probably assistance, transport and premises). How does counselling relate to these examples, if at all? Is there some way of estimating the social utility of counselling and therefore its fair economic rank? We might say that counselling, being concerned with the most fundamental of issues of human welfare, should rank very highly. Alternatively, if counselling is associated with friendship, with a love of one's fellow human beings, then we might object that no price can be put on it, and certainly not a high price.

A valued and skilled service deserves a suitably high rate of remuneration, runs one argument. Connect this with the belief that counsellors are highly trained and skilled, that they show self-respect by valuing themselves and that this transmits itself to clients. Indeed it is the case that some clients will feel reassured by high fees and may assume that better counselling or therapy is available from those who charge higher fees. There are also some practitioners who resent others charging low fees which, in effect, undercut their own fees; so the market rate to some extent tends to reflect an average expectation.

On the other hand, we know that some critics accuse counsellors of acting like mercenaries or 'ambulance chasers'. We know from published accounts that some clients who have paid for years of psychotherapy have come to feel that they've wasted their money, which is not refundable. Counsellors cannot guarantee to 'cure' a client's specific problem, and within a specified time frame.

Against these considerations, what should counsellors in private practice charge? What moral gauge, if any, could be used to help determine this? If a fair income is about £30K and we then allow for all complex and hidden costs, a fair hourly rate for a full-time private practitioner might be, say, £35–£45. 'I do my best and believe £40 an hour is a fair rate,' seems a reasonable conclusion. (These figures are illustrative only.) It's impossible to be definitive because of hidden variable overheads but we should urge clients as consumers to ask what they're actually getting for their money. I know someone who paid a psychologist £80 an hour for several sessions, focusing on panic attacks, that left her feeling no better, and she could have had twice as much time with a counsellor at £40 per hour. I have also known a psychotherapist (very well qualified, and in an imposing detached house) who was charging someone £100 a session with no discernible results. These are anecdotal but accurate observations that will not show up in most research.

If you aim to make your livelihood from counselling, of course you have to work out what you need to live on and work backwards from there to a fair hourly rate. But unfortunately this does not equate with what each client actually gets. Nor does it – unless you can operate a sliding scale – allow clients who are on low incomes to use your service. Personally, I do not consider it moral to charge high fees for counselling or psychotherapy in order to support an affluent lifestyle, especially if you exploit the tacit and unproven belief among some that higher fees mean a better service. Of course, not everyone will agree with this, and there is no external, objective arbiter to decide on such matters.

Further reading

Tudor, K. & Worrall, M. (2002) The unspoken relationship: financial dynamics in freelance therapy. In J. Clark (ed.), *Freelance Counselling and Psychotherapy: Competition and Collaboration*. London: Brunner-Routledge.

Whatever Happened to Self-analysis, Co-counselling, Group and Social Therapy?

The dominant form of counselling and psychotherapy is the face-to-face, one-to-one, asymmetrical and 'professional' one. A counsellor or therapist provides a service to another, known as the client (or sometimes the patient or analysand). But there are other ways of helping and being helped. Friendship is perhaps the primary one but is usually found to be problematic because a friend is tempted to advise or rescue you, wants to say what she would do, isn't necessarily confidential and so on. Let's look at some others and at what can be learned.

Self-analysis, practised by and good enough for Freud, has been advocated as a useful tool for trainees and indeed for anyone. Any of us can try to analyse our own dreams, for example, to keep a journal of our daily experiences, obstacles and behaviour patterns, set ourselves goals and document our progress. In fact many do just this, often with the help of self-help books. Increasingly, people are also offered computer-assisted, packaged therapeutic programmes like 'Beating the Blues'. Therapeutic writing is preferred by some who may have various difficulties accessing face-to-face services. But self-analysis or self-help is dependent on self-discipline and one's own efforts, and lacks the dimension of feedback, encouragement and challenge from another. As the joke goes, 'The only problem with self-analysis is the counter-transference'.

Co-counselling possesses different traditions but all of these revolve around the principle of one person counselling another, and then the roles being switched. Some basic training and an understanding of the groundrules are necessary but co-counselling essentially requires no more than two people willing to help each other to the best of their ability. Co-counselling entails no payments and can proceed by mutual agreement, addressing any issues and taking as long as both agree to participate. Co-counselling remains a fairly widespread activity, usually linked with one organization or another. The beauty of it is that it is 'the people's therapy'. However, there are no guarantees of skill or ethics, and it is possible that people may get out of their depth. One partner may get deeper into painful material than the other, or one might want to carry on longer than the other. There may be no good way of resolving any interpersonal problems that arise. It is possible to arrange for a group of like-minded people to co-counsel, and to switch roles from time to time. Co-counselling has never become as popular as hoped. This may or may not be due to its intrinsic limitations. We could all arrange to cut each other's hair to save on hairdressing costs but the results might not be to our liking.

Group therapy of one kind or another has been practised almost as long as individual therapy but has never become nearly as popular. Group therapy should be cheaper and has the benefits of seeing that others wrestle with problems like one's own; a sense of solidarity and support is common in group therapies. Often there is a strong sense of commitment, as you air your concerns and intentions in front of others. While not group therapy as such, mutual help groups in the addictions field have the strengths associated with common problems and avoid the trappings of professionalized therapies. On the other hand, there are many groups that are facilitated professionally by therapists, some of these with a wide-spectrum agenda, others with specific foci such as eating disorders, anger management or low self-esteem. The disadvantages of group therapies revolve mainly around there being less individual attention, potentially a more confusing variety of inputs, and more compromised confidentiality. Fairly or not, most clients vote with their feet and prefer one-to-one counselling with a professional counsellor or therapist.

Social therapies is a rather vague phrase but here I mean all those attempts to get people to engage with their community therapeutically. Individual therapy suggests that our problems are 'in our heads' and it is our personal responsibility to change. Experiments have been made to involve people in therapeutic community theatre and other projects, to be active and community-oriented rather than merely to talk about the sources of distress and individual aspirations. There is much current discussion abut ecotherapy, for example, and a recognition of links between economic and consumer trends and individual depression. In spite of a great deal of theoretical interest however (and some historical experiments), in practical terms social therapies have not materialized or consolidated.

Other therapy-related endeavours outside the usual one-to-one kind include outward bound projects, meditation, creative writing, self-hypnosis, the spiritually oriented and consumer or user groups dedicated to agitating for improved services. The self-help book market remains strong, suggesting that many identify themselves as needing to change, perhaps as having faith in such literature or lacking the resources to pay for individual therapy. The UK government's Increasing Access to Psychological Therapies (IAPT) programme aspires to offer choices, including telephone and group therapies. Overall, however, at least in our era, people have clearly preferred the privacy and professionalism of traditional one-to-one, face-to-face counselling. This seems to mirror a lack of meaningful politics or powerful protest movements, and the pursuit of individual self-interest – perhaps, too, the need for intimate personal discussion in an increasingly pressurized, dehumanized world.

Further reading

Kauffman, K. & New, C. (2004) *Co-Counselling: The Theory and Practice of Re-evaluation Counselling.* London: Routledge.
Salerno, S. (2006) *Self-Help and Actualization Movement (SHAM).* London: Nicholas Brealey.

Are we Counselling on a Dying Planet?

Three questions are, I think, embedded in this one: (1) Is the planet dying? (2) If the planet is dying, does that mean anything in particular for counselling? (3)

If there is a meaningful link here, what is it and what should we do? First, it seems incontrovertible according to most scientific evidence that man-made climate change, resource depletion and other environmental trends are leading towards a very seriously damaged environment; some, however, would qualify this by stating that the earth will take care of itself but billions of human beings may perish. Second, if things are this bad, can they be rectified in time? Some give us mere decades until a tipping point, while others are hopeful of finding technological solutions for carbon reduction. I will come on to the implications for counselling presently. Third, there are many links for counselling, again to be outlined below.

According to some accounts, we human beings have been living beyond our environmental means for millennia, there being clear connections between the development of agriculture, industry, massive and untenable population expansion and anthropogenic environmental damage. This hasn't resulted only in external damage but also in damage to our own psyches, as we have become alienated from nature itself and mostly live unnatural lives in overcrowded cities. This very way of life is a contributing factor in compromised mental health. Our global capitalist economies depend on continuous growth, which means untenable carbon emissions. We are all enmeshed in a counterproductive way of living and working, and only drastic changes in an austere direction can remedy matters. If we or our politicians don't act swiftly and radically, climate change is inevitable, which will lead to rising sea levels and flooding, many parts of the world becoming uninhabitable, drought and famine, disease, mass migration and violence.

Counselling is a small-scale, usually one-to-one, inward looking activity. Usually anyone's personal distress is more important to them than political or environmental matters. But clearly, if potential disaster is mere decades away, counsellors and others can be accused of fiddling while Rome burns or rearranging deckchairs on the *Titanic*. Clearly, if climate change predictions have any accuracy (not to mention pressures on the national budget due to economic recession), then funding for counselling is unlikely to be a top priority. It would probably be irresponsible to argue for increased funding when climatological research and carbon reduction technology would have axiomatically greater claims to make. People might suffer psychologically but if human life itself is on the line, and the lives of our children, then the priorities are surely clear. In addition to this, we have to envisage possible worst case scenarios. Some are already planning for the possibilities mentioned above, such as increased famine and disease, the desperate migration that follows and the violence surrounding it. Another component in this scenario is population control, and counselling might have some role to play in helping people come to terms with radically altered expectations.

Now, of course two common responses to all this are (1) these are the unfounded pessimistic visions of doomsayers, and (2) there is little if anything counselling can do about all this, and it is not in the remit of counsellors directly to address such issues or involve clients in them. I believe it is far from being a lunatic fringe that is making dire forecasts, the Intergovernmental Panel on Climate Change (IPCC) itself being a major source of such information. Concern about these matters is rational. Images of environmental degradation affect us all through the media, and clients as well as we ourselves are affected psychologically.

There is a distinct danger that if we remain myopically fixated on the professional survival agenda for counselling we will miss the bigger picture. This applies not only to counselling but also to many other agendas. But at the heart of counselling lies a concern with human welfare and wellbeing. Maslow's hierarchy of needs has often formed part of counselling training but we have taken it for granted that physical needs have been satisfied (in the West at least). It looks like we should not be taking these for granted any longer.

On what level should these matters enter our awareness and affect counselling practice? Some publications already tackle them, for instance occasional articles about ecotherapy. Professional bodies need to take them into account. In what ways should they enter the curricula of training courses? This may be problematic because topics vie for space on courses already. How – if at all – should they enter into practice? Probably they will arise spontaneously anyway and should not be forced. We probably need to start thinking about implications and roles. How, in the coming years, might we concretely experience climate change? Older people are at increased risk of death in high summer temperatures, for example. People of childbearing age may think twice about having children. (In fact a small number of young women have opted for voluntary sterilization as a response to such concerns.) It seems highly likely that in spite of uncritically pro-capitalist rhetoric about continuing economic growth, lifestyles will have to adapt. Everyday life could become harsher, or provide fewer escapes (e.g. fewer cheap holidays, less car travel) or possibly 'more human', as people learn to make do with less. Counselling itself might change its nature, to address common adaptation needs.

Further reading

Rowe, D. (1987) Avoiding the big issues and attending to the small. In S. Fairbairn and G. Fairbairn (eds), *Psychology, Ethics and Change*. London: Routledge and Kegan Paul.

Counselling, Society and Culture:

Counselling is primarily based on the individual person in distress and on what goes on in her or his head, and on what can be talked about. Counselling has been criticized for over-psychologizing problems in living and ignoring the social realities in which we are embedded. To some extent we address particular areas of diversity and oppression but arguably most training (and practice?) fails to consider socio-cultural factors. Must we accept that counselling is in fact an individual-centred activity that cannot make any inroads on social problems? Reflect on where you think you belong in society and what the implications are. Are you somewhat conservative in your views or impassioned about wider social problems? Some would even say that counselling as a movement and profession is complicit in a capitalist society that routinely causes distress. Consider the arguments against that view.

Reading

Morrall, P. (2009) *The Trouble with Therapy: Sociology and Psychotherapy.* Maidenhead: Open University Press.

Pauline has been a counsellor for twenty years, working in various settings. She has favoured work in the voluntary sector where she can see clients on low incomes who often have multiple problems. Politically, she has always held left-wing views. Recently she has become very concerned about local unemployment, national economics and environmental problems. Pauline enjoys her counselling but wants to spend more time being politically active. She has tried to find concrete links between counselling and politics but has struggled with this endeavour. She does not have a high income herself and realizes that her pension will not amount to much when she retires. Is there any way in which she can combine her interests? Should she compromise herself and find better paid work with better pension provision? Do you consider counselling apolitical or can it (and should it) be shaped more towards social change? (See Samuels, 1993.)

Critical thinking perspectives

Pauline could be seen as an unsung hero who has immersed herself in valuable work that, however satisfying, has not put her in a good financial position, and nor can it satisfy all her aspirations. She finds herself in midlife struggling to make satisfying vocational changes. It's quite possible she might find work that includes the use of counselling and socio-political awareness. However, in spite of many attempts to strengthen political insights for therapists, there appears to be very little in the way of occupational initiatives in this area; even critical psychologists may struggle to find roles that combine political activism with clinical work – unless people like Pauline were willing to travel to the USA and other places to work as social therapists in the manner of Newman (2003). Alternatively, she might find small ways of injecting political awareness into her counselling work. Ultimately, however, people like Pauline are never likely to be (and perhaps do not want to be) in a strong financial position.

Spiritual and
Philosophical Issues

Does Counselling Rest on Faith and Hope?

Both faith and hope have religious connotations, although it is not necessary to be religious in order to invest in them. Faith implies a belief in something that is often intangible and may be longstanding. Hope suggests a wish for something better to happen in the future. It is possible to benefit from medication even without faith, or to win the lottery without faith. It is possible to maintain a faith and hope in religion without any manifestations of a tangible change or result. It is unlikely however that anyone would become a counsellor without some degree of faith in counselling, or that a client would enter or persevere in counselling without some hope. One need not be *strongly* optimistic in order to have some faith in counselling, since faith can be no more than willingness to try – a 'let's see' attitude.

Faith, implying loyalty and a certain 'sticking with' something through doubts and setbacks, may sit well with some counsellors but is likely to arouse questions. It too readily chimes with 'faith healing', for example, with the principle that counselling may be some sort of wishful thinking, voodoo-like activity. Even those who eschew a scientific identity for counselling may not welcome a faith identity instead. On the other hand, understood as faith in human beings, in their essential goodness, strength and ability to find – and to have an entitlement to – a better life, the concept of faith probably has wide acceptance.

Faith can be contrasted with hope. There are people, sometimes called therapy-junkies, who take on a belief in counselling or therapy, and personal growth, that resembles an evangelical religion. They 'eat, drink and breathe' therapy; they talk about it, read about it, attend endless workshops and live a life saturated in therapy themes. I am not sure if this is healthy. It is like a substitute life. Spending some period of your life with a strong commitment to and fascination with therapy is understandable and can be helpful. There is a Zen Buddhist parable about the man who uses a raft to cross a river and then takes the raft everywhere with him, worshipping it. He has misunderstood the point of the raft, which is to provide temporary assistance. It may be best on the whole if such therapeutic faith is temporary.

But presumably faith for the counsellor must be permanent? What would happen if a counsellor lost their faith in counselling? We have very few such accounts but we can assume such losses do happen, as they do in religion when a priest finds he can no longer sustain his original faith. He usually cannot simply walk out on his vocation since he may need time to digest the change and to find an alternative livelihood. It seems unlikely that counsellors will retain across decades the level of faith they probably felt on initially embracing counselling. Some might and others might not, but we should expect to see some changes in attitude. We might ask what this means for the clients of counsellors who have been practising for many years. We could infer that the claim that some beginning counsellors compare very favourably with more experienced practitioners may be based on this phenomenon. Counselling rests on faith but that faith may diminish in intensity, at least for some.

What about hope? We can assume that some degree of hope is present in all new counselling relationships. Even the depressed person who has had counselling before must have some smidgen of hope that this time things will be different. Even the counsellor who quickly realizes how chronically depressed a client is must hope that she can effect some change. Now, it is possible to suspend both hope and hopelessness if you are able to enter a certain meditative state – something like Bion's 'without memory or desire' – while paying attention fully to the present and (in the best sense) expecting nothing. But we also know that different personalities harbour or give up on hope in different ways. Hope may come and go, like any mood, although some people will have more than their fair share of sustained hope or protracted despair.

It's possible to think in terms of a combined scientific-and-mystical attitude to discovery that transcends faith and hope. Instead it seeks to suspend expectation, to study objectively. Both faith and hope are psychological states containing emotional components. Faith may bludgeon on through moods of doubt, hanging on to memory and dogma; hope may grasp a vision of the day when obstacles will fall away, when things will finally fall into place. Both could be rewarded, insofar as persistence and patience can sometimes pay off. Counselling does seem to rest on these twin pillars. But ultimately perhaps they must give way to an openness to whatever may be. Ultimately there are no guarantees of happy or dramatically positive outcomes, only that what is, is.

Further reading

Halmos, P. (1965) *The Faith of the Counsellors*. London: Constable.

39

Are Life, Training and Counselling Part of a 'Journey'?

The journey metaphor is used so often that it must have some widespread resonance and bear some analysis. I hear it at interviews, in classes, in the media, all around me, certainly among students of counselling but also more generally. This 'journey' seems to have romantic, spiritual and mysterious connotations. 'It is better to travel than to arrive' is part of its mystique. It's as if every day is a new challenge and we can't know what's around the corner. Yet most of those who use the term appear outwardly to have quite settled, unadventurous lives and I am left wondering what they actually mean. Could they have a secret existence? Are they imagining things? Is their inner life much richer than their outer one? Sometimes those who use this term appear to mean that, looking back on their lives, they would not have imagined they'd be where they are today – married to *this* person, living in *this* place, doing *this* job and *this* training course. I do not know if they are referring to paragliding activities, bungee jumping, safaris, unusual sex, drugs, or other extreme adventures. Perhaps increased social mobility and a widening participation in higher education have led to this feeling that people are doing things their parents would not have dreamed of doing.

Much more subtly, however, they may be talking simply about the way they feel. Since spirituality is such a commonly used phrase today as well, perhaps those on a journey mean that they are in touch with subtle inner energies, psychic paths and so on. Tempted to mockery though I sometimes am, I am also partly plain curious about what is meant by these terms and their prevalence. Presumably 'I am on a journey' or 'life is a journey' distinguishes between some other phase of life when life didn't feel that way, when it was boring, dreary, linear and stuck. Being on a journey has a sense of excitement about it, about sharpened senses and a keen perception, about an openness to new experiences. It could also mean that since my divorce, or bereavement, redundancy or other turmoil, I choose not to see myself as damaged but as changing course and taking a new, unknown direction. This may or may not be part of a defence against pain.

Another possible interpretation of the term 'journey' is that it means very little at all, perhaps nothing. The erstwhile comment on life – 'Perhaps it's all a dream' (not heard so much now) – had the qualities of wistfulness and disillusionment and revealed a sense of puzzlement, as if that which should be so obvious and grounded had turned out to be elusive and slightly threatening. The journey metaphor seems to be wishful, future-oriented, expectant. Does the latter suggest we are in a new era? Is it a good sign of a collective optimism or a delusion? Or could it simply be a sloppy linguistic usage, similar to the phrase 'It's all about the relationship'? Do people feel that their lives are really in a hopeful transition, that they are going somewhere better, however vague? If so, it does feel different from the quagmire or wasteland metaphors of previous decades. Could it express a sense that all is movement, that just as international travel is cheap and accessible to all, so reincarnation may mean that other lives always await us? You can easily hop on a plane to Prague or Bangkok, and who knows – you might walk into an unexpected new relationship, a new lifestyle, a transformational illness or a better incarnation. In fact, the 'journey' isn't necessarily all positive or rosy, as it can contain darkness and threat, but that too can at least be interesting and lead to further learning.

Metaphors, slogans or ideas about movement – personal development, continuing professional development, becoming, going forward, moving on, hitting the ground running, moving with the times – are obviously not static. The idea of a spiritual journey implies movement too, in contrast with the principle of stillness, the 'still point in a turning world' aligned with meditation, with acceptance in the midst of turmoil and turbulence. In counselling training, do people discover more and more about themselves, or might they become more and more acceptant of what simply is, of who they are? Is there some optimal condition between or above either being stuck or forever hoping for a better destination? Given that human beings can be inclined to an uncritical repetition of empty feelgood buzzwords, it seems important we should stop to ask what actual freshness, meaning and limitations the journey metaphor has in counselling circles.

Further reading

Bays, B. (1999) *The Journey.* Northampton: Thorsons.
Lydon, W.J., Clay, A.L. & Sparks, C.L. (2001) Metaphor and change in counseling. *Journal of Counseling and Development,* 79 (3), 269–274.

Can Counselling make you Enlightened?

Enlightenment is one of the names given to a state of supreme freedom from the typical human experience of being preoccupied with troubles and suffering. There are a variety of terms for this and these overlap between different religions in shades of meaning. The best known example is the Buddha, who is said to have become enlightened – freed once and for all from unnecessary suffering – while meditating under a tree. This experience followed Gautama Buddha's awareness of the ubiquity of suffering and his trial and error search for a genuine way out of it. At that time and place (about five hundred years before Christ, in Nepal) Gautama could access various teachers, often hermits, who practised ascetic lifestyles and meditated in the hope of transcending normal, problematic human consciousness. He seems finally to have attained enlightenment by some mixture of exhausting the search through others, persistently looking inwards and perhaps sheer chance. Kirschner (1996) also gives many compelling examples of links between psychoanalysis and the 'Christian mystical narrative' of the Fall and reunion.

In case any readers see no obvious connections between this outline and the work of our contemporary counsellors and therapists, let me suggest some. Even two-and-a-half thousand years ago human beings in a far less populated and urbanized time consciously knew suffering, at least in the forms of ageing, disease, hardship and dying. That suffering seemed universal. Buddhism also contains descriptions of many subtle psychological forms of suffering that we today might recognize as neuroses or disorders. The Buddha taught that the mind is commonly restless and involved in desire and fear: we constantly want what we do not have and want to avoid those things we imagine will bring us pain. Some central activity in the human mind itself is responsible for generating unease – anxiety, depression, envy, regret and so on. In our world we have many competing theories about the sources of and remedies for our psychological suffering but some of them apparently broadly agree with the Buddhist analysis in identifying self-defeating thoughts as key. However, there is at least one glaring problem with trying to equate modern therapies with original Buddhism: while Gautama seems to have become and remained enlightened or wholly liberated, nowadays we have few if any examples of people who have been similarly freed by counselling and psychotherapy.

Several objections can be raised to the picture I paint here. Some will justifiably argue that we have no evidence whatsoever that this man Gautama the Buddha actually attained the state of enlightenment. Some will say that such a state may not exist at all. Even if he did, and there is such a state, we might also argue that it is unique or extremely rare, that it may be an outcome of spiritual or mystical genius. We can easily observe that although founders of spiritual movements may have had such experiences themselves, their followers seem to have struggled to attain anything like enlightenment (or supreme wisdom, grace or whatever term we care to use). Sometimes women raise the natural objection that all such claims are associated with men, and involve apparently 'intrapsychic' experience rather than relational improvements. Certainly we can observe practitioners of long-term meditation and psychoanalysis who do not appear to have reached anything likeenlightenment. Yet others would argue that enlightenment as an 'end goal' is mythical and a misunderstanding – that freedom and maturity come as small, transient, undramatic increments.

Many further objections can be made to the notion of enlightenment but it looks as if a few modern people like Ramana Maharshi, Jiddu Krishnamurti, U.G. Krishnamurti and perhaps Eckhart Tolle have attained it and tried to help others towards it. Often an enlightenment narrative contains features of acute involuntary suffering, a re-experiencing of previous life events, a powerful catharsis and mental stillness, followed by a permanent state of freedom from habitual thought and an ability to live fully in the present. My point here is that if such a state genuinely exists we would surely be interested in it, and arguably that all counselling and psychotherapy theory ultimately points towards questions about the source of mental anguish or suffering and its elimination, and then towards an optimal state of human functioning. Indeed most humanistic psychology theorists and practitioners have called forth just such visions. Some modern cognitive therapy now incorporates mindfulness training as a therapeutic component.

However, I have heard of no claims to or observations of enlightenment in the world of counselling and psychotherapy. Many people will say they feel better, and a relative few will choose to dedicate themselves to the pursuit of ever higher levels of consciousness. But there seems to be little if any evidence for any of this. Unfortunately there may also be reasons to suspect that some who have been involved in transpersonal therapies may be deluding themselves and/or deceiving others. Bhagwan Shree Rajneesh (or Osho), for example, launched a movement blending meditational, spiritual dance, free love and therapeutic techniques that ended in ignominy. Scientology is constructed along blended religious-therapeutic lines with the notion of an ascending consciousness. Several transpersonal therapies aim at higher states of consciousness and many in the counselling world like to speak of themselves as spiritual. They may not be promising enlightenment but there is an implied movement towards ever higher or better consciousness.

The short answer to my question, 'Can counselling make you enlightened?' is unfortunately 'No'. There is no formal evidence for it and little if any anecdotal evidence exists. Even if we argue that counselling cannot *make* anyone anything, but only facilitate or guide, we still have no grounds for believing that anyone incidentally becomes enlightened via counselling. Rather, almost universally, users of counselling of all kinds (or psychotherapy or psychoanalysis) achieve quite modest results. These are no doubt worthwhile freedoms from some aspects of suffering but in no way do they constitute a holistic, permanent liberation from common human woe.

Further reading

Epstein, M. (1996) *Thoughts Without a Thinker: Psychotherapy from a Buddhist Perspective.* London: Duckworth.

Trasi, N. (1999) *The Science of Enlightenment.* New Delhi: D.K. Printworld.

Young-Eisendrath, P. & Muramoto, S. (eds) (2002) *Awakening and Insight: Zen Buddhism and Psychotherapy.* London: Brunner-Routledge.

Whatever Happened to Free Will and Willpower?

In a nutshell, the problem of will is this – that we often know what we need to do, that is, what's good for us, but we fail to do it. While some clients commence counselling confused, many already know what they need to do, or soon realize, but then will procrastinate. We may need to do something decisively beneficial (such as exercising) or stop doing something self-harmful (such as over-eating), we resolve to take appropriate action and may even do so, but commonly we lose impetus and relapse. This is well recognized in the idea of cycles of change. But if will is so critical a topic in counselling, why does it not appear more frequently in counselling texts?

The concept of will also appears as willpower, free will and conation, and can imply motivation, desire, intentionality, self-control, effort, even force. It is evident in writings from St Paul to Schopenhauer and Nietzsche, if with very different connotations. It has been extensively studied by psychologists and is recommended by some existentialist therapists like Frankl and May. Otto Rank created 'will therapy', which soon lost favour and was even associated with Nazism. Gestalt therapy sometimes reframes 'I can't' in terms of 'I won't' and rational emotive behaviour therapy commends the constant practice of new behaviour. If we generalize will to something like a life force or drive, we see it in the actualizing tendency of person-centred therapy and in the eros of psychoanalysis. But equally we can see its dark side in folk psychology and philosophy, as in the concepts of weakness of will, paralysis of the will and wilfulness, and in the perennial debate on free will and determinism. Obviously, we can sometimes will ourselves to do or cease something but not always successfully. Less obviously, we are usually physically free to leave an unsatisfactory job or relationship but seldom without turmoil, and often economic circumstances and emotional pull, and social censure, will seem too overpowering to resist.

On the positive side, the concept of will – and reminding clients that they do have some free will – shows that change is often directly in our hands: we *can* go to the gym, resist the cigarette or cake and so on. On the negative side, will may seem like a mere suppression of internal conflict or struggling with a habit. Many would argue that insight and understanding have to precede willed action or that action flows naturally from insight. When examined closely, it is clear that there is really no 'will' in mental isolation from our bodies. We may try to suppress the bodily craving for nicotine, sugar, alcohol or sex, for example, but the underlying physiological force often feels stronger than our conscious resolution. In other words, a split between body and mind is apparent. Indeed it has been argued that our minds are so constructed that they must present us with an illusion of executive will. Anorexics will exercise their control over hunger and workaholics over the need for a rest and life balance. It looks like some individuals have too much and others too little will, or self-control, so that applying the same therapeutic expectations to all will not work. It is also fairly clear that while actions can sometimes be readily willed, feelings cannot: I cannot genuinely will myself to love someone or to feel happy. I can however will small constructive acts that will cumulatively make me feel self-efficacious and less depressed, which is the essence of cognitive therapy.

Sometimes we simply feel good, and free of conflict, and we need no conscious will or the illusion of will. Particularly after some cathartic experience in counselling, or after meditation, a window of spontaneous freedom or 'flow' may appear. But this rarely lasts. Short-term will may need to give way to a longer-term commitment to positive life goals and along the way we should realistically expect setbacks. Perhaps counsellors can point clients to those areas of their lives where they have the choice to exercise will and when they seem to be denying this unhelpfully. Counsellors probably need to recognize personality types and where these stand in relation to strength of will. In some cases clients may be reacting to having parents' or teachers' wills imposed on them and need to regain ownership of and respect for their own will.

Is the concept of will useful or necessary in counselling? Does it help clients? To what degree are we free to decide and act against bodily impulses, moods, habits and inertia? Should will appear more in counselling texts and our field be better informed by philosophical and neurological perspectives on will? Or are these redundant, old-fashioned and imprecise concepts?

Further reading

Wegner, D.M. (2002) *The Illusion of Conscious Will*. Cambridge, MA: Bradford.
Charlton, W. (1988) *Weakness of Will: A Philosophical Introduction*. Oxford: Blackwell.
Wilks, D. (2003) A historical review of counseling theory development in relation to definitions of free will and determinism. *Journal of Counseling and Development,* 81 (3), 278–284.

Do we Need to Have a View about the World/Reality/Existence Itself?

Most clients will go to counselling with some crisis or everyday concern and probably seek quite practical or emotional ways forward. Probably most counsellors do not see any need for an explicit worldview in their work. Existential counselling does rest on thought through worldviews (or *Weltanschauungen*) and considers it important that clients explore their own in order to facilitate a decisional and change process. I have heard counsellors expressing impatience with the idea that reflecting on ostensibly philosophical matters has any real value for counselling practice. Let's look at this.

One view about the universe is that it came about randomly or accidentally, and all that followed is also random, without any design or purpose. Another is that God created the universe and everything in it, that He looks over it and everything within it has a purpose. Some want to paint existence and human life in metaphorical terms as a journey, an odyssey, a path that individuals make by their own moral, even heroic actions. Some remain agnostic about all these matters (after all, we have no final answers yet) but draw attention to more urgent social and psychological matters. My guess is that a majority of counsellors belong mainly to this latter group, perhaps with some believing in a vaguely spiritual purpose.

Personally, I have a very amateur interest in cosmology, have studied theology and read widely. On most days I will peruse a newspaper. I have assumed that this is normal and healthy, perhaps even essential. But on meeting a counsellor who said she never read newspapers and had little idea what was going on in the world, I wondered if I was right. Does it make any difference to engage in wider questions about the world, reality and existence? Must you be a philosopher to ask such questions? Is there any reason to think you may be an inferior counsellor if you never or rarely formulate views about these matters?

The term 'philosophical empathy' refers to an ability to understand another's views about the world. We readily accept the value of striving to understand a client's most subjective world, her subtle inner feelings and meanings, from moment to moment. But could it be almost as important to understand a client's assumptions about the nature of reality? We may believe this is a dog eat dog world, a meaningless vale of tears, a moral test or comical circus of events and relationships. We may believe that life is or should be fair, that if you act honourably others should, and will, too. Some believe that a heaven or paradise awaits them as long as they behave strictly according to religious moral precepts. Others believe simply that life is short and what you make it, so it's better to eat, drink and be merry. Clients who hold any of these views may be sustained by them or deeply disappointed when their expectations are not met.

In a sense the painful symptoms of post-traumatic stress disorder (PTSD) attest to the violent rupture that occurs in an accident or disaster that shatters our expectations of continuity and fairness. Disruptive and random, unfair events (so perceived) often lead to feelings of terrible chaos and confusion: 'I cannot cope, I cannot carry on, in a world so unpredictable and unfair'. Alternatively, some people cope very well by relying on their religious beliefs: God moves in mysterious ways, there must be some unknown purpose behind this tragedy, and so on. Victor Frankl is famous for stating that those holding a strong belief in some higher purpose survived concentration camps better than those who did not. And many alcoholics have found help in Alcoholics Anonymous' appeal to a higher being.

It seems that *what* people believe in matters little, unless it is some sort of precarious or self-persecutory belief. Should it matter if a client feels reassured by a belief in flying saucers, astrological predictions or whatever? Does it matter if you believe in creationist theories instead of geological and evolutionary evidence? (Does it matter if my client is a creationist and I am a Darwinian?) Conflicts – muted or open – could occur. I may believe that life is random and painful and hardly worth the effort of living: is this as acceptable as creationism, or more or less acceptable?

A common answer to such questions is that it is the client's reality that counts above all, and it must be honoured and worked with. Person-centred counsellors in particular hold such views. Some psychodynamic counsellors may regard certain improbable beliefs held by clients as defence mechanisms that will weaken and fade in time, with counselling and an acceptance of the pain that drove them. Yet others may attempt to accept the client but bracket their improbable views during counselling. Again, does it matter which position the counsellor takes?

Comparable with the counsellor who reads no newspapers, is it OK for counsellors to know nothing about the universe, about evolution and human history, to have no sense of the timescale of human evolution and no knowledge of evolutionary psychology? Many counsellors are suspicious of science and may prefer religious and astrological explanations for world and personal events. Is that acceptable? We can ask whether counsellors should be well informed and have good general knowledge, but it may be that a knowledge of a client's inner world and local culture is more helpful than a knowledge of human history and sociology, for example. Curiously (to my mind), we can agonize about the necessity of clinical supervision (and even pore critically over connotations of terms like 'clinical') while ignoring or marginalizing these bigger questions.

Further reading

Messer, S.B. (1992) A critical examination of belief structures in integrative and eclectic psychotherapy. In J.C. Norcross & M.R. Goldfried (eds), *Handbook of Psychotherapy Integration*. New York: Basic Books.

Reker, G.T. & Chamberlain, K. (eds) (2000) *Exploring Existential Meaning*. Thousand Oaks, CA: Sage.

Spiritual and Philosophical Issues:

Many counsellors individually, and advocates of some therapeutic approaches, consider themselves 'spiritual' but do not always articulate well the basis of this claim. Certainly some critics of counselling regard it as a ragbag of poorly explicated, woolly ideas. Is it fair to criticize counselling and counsellors on these grounds? Would training be improved by incorporating more explicitly an examination of spiritual claims and philosophical perspectives (Howard, 2000)?

Reading

Howard, A. (2000) *Philosophy for Counselling and Psychotherapy: Pythagoras to Postmodernism*. Basingstoke: Macmillan.

Sarah sees a counsellor, Sebastian, who has a distinguished reputation in the region as a wise spiritual counsellor. After three years she begins to wonder whether his occasional lateness, sleepiness and eccentric manner are the forgivable idiosyncrasies of an otherwise quite enlightened man. But she is still in awe of him and tends to ask herself what defences against deeper spiritual realization may be involved in the way she doubts him. Occasionally when she dares to raise doubts, Sebastian laughs, his eyes twinkle and she melts. How can Sarah know if she is making progress and if her persistence will pay off? Can she trust her feelings or is there any third party or other source of advice she can access? (See Zweig & Abrams, 1991.)

Critical thinking perspectives

It is possible to think of Sebastian's behaviour and manner as real, and as more genuine and significant than everyday clinical boundaries and expectations; it is hard to imagine the 'great' figures of religion filling in membership and accreditation application forms, for example. Perhaps some people *are* 'above all the law', as it were. It's possible that Sarah is defensive, engaging in a retreat into anxiety about 'normal behaviour' (or that in seeking spiritual experience she was avoiding some more concrete pain within herself). On the other hand, some people do get hurt by cults and intensive asymmetrical relationships, and some guru-like counsellors and therapists have been known to exploit clients. Who can be the 'monitor' of such situations – the professional body? We might stand back even further and suggest that the individual's reality is paramount, not the assertions and illusions of professions and spiritualities: ultimately only Sarah can decide.

Counselling Wisdom

Is Counselling Non-directive and Value-free?

Part of the tradition of counselling has been that it is 'neutral' as to general values, or rather that, in entering the client's own internal frame of reference and being non-directive, the counsellor strives not to influence the client to take any particular decision or course of action. This has often been interpreted to mean that while the counsellor may hold certain political, religious or therapeutic views, he or she will suspend these and address only those topics and aims chosen by the client. This remains the orthodox belief, that is, that this is both ethically correct and practically possible. But is it?

It's been pointed out that even Carl Rogers, strenuously trying to avoid influencing the client, would nod and make encouraging noises when clients said something he approved of, for example giving non-verbal approval to client statements about the goodness of authenticity and autonomy. So, one question here is whether counsellors' views can be concealed. Perhaps alongside this is the question of whether certain views and values are potentially more influential and more effort should be made to conceal them. These examples are from the person-centred approach but a psychodynamic counsellor would probably deflect or reframe statements (for different reasons) so that clients would not be influenced.

'What do you think I should do?' is a not uncommon question from clients. The person-centred counsellor wants to sidestep the question so that the client learns the value of self-determination. The psychodynamic counsellor might want to focus on the client's anxiety and its roots in a dependency on parents. Counsellors are also aware that advice-giving is not their role and can, if given, backfire when it goes wrong. They also know that clients are very ready to imagine that their counsellors have advised them when this is not the case; often this is a mixture of eagerness to project a decision on to another and a misconstrual. We may say it is simply the *intention* of the counsellor to remain non-directive and value-free within counselling but that she or he cannot conceal every thought or prevent the client from drawing conclusions. The counsellor's manner, dress and setting may all give out clues.

What kinds of values might counsellors hold, even if concealed? Presumably all believe in the value of counselling and its ethical guidelines, and all believe in human dignity. By definition most counsellors are likely to be quite liberal in their views, that is, believing that individual choice is usually sacrosanct. It is difficult to imagine that a counsellor would be offended by swearing or be hardline anti-abortion or homophobic, for example. However, some counsellors might have some reservations about misogynistic swearing, abortion in certain circumstances or some sexual practices.

Three possibilities emerge here: (1) the counsellor can be purely and genuinely non-directive and value-free; (2) the counsellor has certain values but manages to conceal them or explicitly refuses to disclose them; (3) the counsellor cannot or does not want to conceal her values. (1) seems a fairly unlikely eventuality, perhaps theoretically possible, (2) is probably the most common practice, and (3) might be considered ethically dubious but is still worth considering more closely.

Counsellors practising according to any distinct model should explain this to clients and also this will contain some value and influence: you cannot practise CBT without demonstrating a belief in the importance of cognition and behaviour, for instance, nor can you practise CBT without being somewhat directive. But similar phenomena can be detected in all other approaches. You cannot go through any form of primal therapy, for example, without commending and even demanding the expression of strong feelings and outspoken honesty, and underpinning these is a belief in the primacy of feelings which contradicts CBT views.

Alcohol counselling agencies do not demand that people stop drinking but at least imply that excessive drinking (and self-destruction) is not a good idea. Counsellors working with anorexic women may consider the view that is sometimes put forward that it is the client's right to decide on her food intake and weight, but ultimately they will hold very strong views about the preservation of health and life. Student counsellors respect the right of each client to decide on whether or not to continue with his or her course of studies but they will be aware of the setting and its norms, and may subtly exert some pressure in favour of 'student retention'.

Certain counsellors working within an explicit religious identity will not hide their belief that abortion and homosexuality are wrong. Indeed some anti-gay Christian counsellors attempt to convert clients from a gay to a heterosexual lifestyle, often with the client's assent. Most openly 'pro-gay' counsellors will presumably want to encourage the client to embrace an unashamed gay identity. Similarly, some feminist counsellors are explicit about their position and may seek to persuade female clients to cease acquiescing with male violence or even male norms of any kind.

Mainstream counselling apparently aspires to being value-free, or at least to the principle of counsellors holding back on their personal or organizational views. This looks like an honourable position genuinely dedicated to client welfare but its many nuances are frequently overlooked.

Further reading

Villas-Boas Bowen, M. (1996) The myth of non-directiveness: the case of Jill. In B.A. Farber, D.C. Brink & P.M. Raskin (eds), *The Psychotherapy of Carl Rogers: Cases and Commentary*. New York: Guilford.

44

Is it All About the Relationship?

In recent years it has become commonplace to state that the therapeutic relationship is *the* key to effective counselling. This is partly based on inferences from early research which found little difference in effectiveness across models: if all are working well in spite of being based on different theories and using different techniques, then other, common factors must be largely responsible for success. These include counsellor-provided non-judgemental warmth and concern and communicated empathy, but also the trust and rapport established between client and counsellor. Obviously if a 'good relationship' is in place, then effective therapy is likely to happen. Or is it, necessarily? It's possible that a good, enjoyable, trusting relationship becomes a substitute for change via challenge and hard work. Of course we can also assume that a full therapeutic relationship includes all necessary elements, the warm as well as the difficult ones.

Something I have long suspected is that when students and colleagues repeat the mantra that it's all about the relationship, they are quite unclear about what they mean. It seems they do usually mean 'warm and trusting' above all – intimate, confiding, rewarding, purposeful. In my experience with supervisees, most can easily say which of their clients they look forward to seeing and working with and which they feel are hard work – aimless, unclear, unco-operative and so on. When both client and counsellor positively appreciate meeting, both feel that counselling is worthwhile and going somewhere. Such counselling may not resolve the issues the client first came with but nevertheless they may feel better – heard, understood, normal, 'held', relieved.

Person-centred and psychodynamic counsellors have the most explicit rationales for working relationally, the former with core conditions (the person- to-person relationship in Clarkson's well known schema) and the latter with transference dynamics. All other practitioners agree that a good enough working relationship must exist that can underpin everything else, but some practitioners of CBT, REBT and NLP, for example, will concentrate on their techniques. The relationship with the client may be primarily a professional, working one. Some approaches working reparatively and regressively with very damaged clients use what Clarkson called the 'developmentally needed relationship'. And some use or 'run into' the transpersonal relationship, containing spiritual phenomena. Sometimes played down are the effects of differences in gender, race and culture, and age and sexuality, as well as personality.

My impression is that counsellors are mostly talking about a good rapport when they say, 'It's all about the relationship'. It may be 'relationally led' but also contain unrecognized ingredients of common personality factors, social and family likenesses, intuition, improvised counselling skills and techniques. It may feel 'natural' rather than an artificial therapeutic exercise. But if it is somewhat rapport-centred, then this implies that it is partly reliant on chance, and we will not get on so easily or help so well those clients with whom we do not have a natural rapport. It is, however, possible to talk about working at a relationship, so that when ruptures or problems occur that are successfully addressed, this may strengthen the relationship – and thus the therapy itself – all the more.

Are we talking here about a total relationship or a visual-and-verbal relationship? Telephone counselling, for example, is often thought to be 'less relational' or less natural because it lacks a visual reality and cues. Psychoanalysis on the couch may be considered not fully relational because the patient/client cannot see the analyst. But where blind clients or therapists are involved there are no visual cues, yet we would not say that these are less relationally rich. There are many examples of unconventional therapeutic relationships, including online counselling. Of course, we are never talking about a total relationship but a professional therapeutic relationship that by its very nature precludes friendship and sex. We also put aside the question of an alienating society and subsequently fragmented relationships that may underpin relational help-seeking through therapy.

One of the greatest of indictments that follow from the belief that successful counselling is all about the relationship is that, if it is, then all those approaches emphasizing skills and techniques are ultimately wasting (at least a lot of) their time. It is different to claim that successful counselling is mainly or partly about a good therapeutic relationship. Perhaps those who make the extravagant claim that 'The relationship is all' really mean that underpinning everything else and after everything else has been tried it is the relationship between client and counsellor that is the foundation and clincher. If we take into account the research claiming that the relationship is responsible for some 30 per cent of successful outcomes, techniques 15 per cent, theory 15 per cent and extra-therapeutic factors 40 per cent (Lambert, 1992), then we can say that the relationship has overall a greater contributory importance than either theory or technique – but it still doesn't justify the 'It's all about the relationship' claim. Above all, the criticism here is about precision and language: what do we mean *exactly* when we say, 'It's all about the relationship'? It seems to me that it is obviously not *all* about the relationship, that it is also largely about the client's motivation and the personality match and awareness between the two people involved – but it is hard, indeed perhaps impossible, to say in each case what percentage of significance can be attributed to different variables.

Further reading

Clarkson, P. (2003) *The Therapeutic Relationship* (2nd edn). London: Whurr.
Feltham, C. (ed.) (1999) *Understanding the Counselling Relationship*. London: Sage.
Knox, R. (2008) Clients' experiences of relational depth in person-centred counselling. *Counselling and Psychotherapy Research,* 8 (3), 182–188.
Slife, B. & Wiggins, B.J. (2009) Taking relationship seriously in psychotherapy: radical relationality. *Journal of Contemporary Psychotherapy,* 39 (1), 17–24.

Does the Client Know Best?

It is quite commonly asserted that the client knows best, the client is the expert, the task of the counsellor is merely to help the client to access and trust her own internal frame of reference. It is the client's life, the client's own values and needs are paramount, all human beings are reliably self-directing, and most problems have come from people being unwisely pushed and misdirected by others. So runs typical counselling wisdom, much of this originating from the thought of Carl Rogers.

This sentiment has a certain romantic and democratic charm to it. We are all equal, all worthy of respect, our lives are our own to live. 'Live (as you would like to) and let others live (as they would like to)' runs the folk wisdom. If we were all treated with respect and trusted, all would be well. The glaring flaw in this statement, however, as many have pointed out, is that if clients know best, how come so many of them (of us) have messed up large areas of their lives? How come they are so much in need of help from others like counsellors?

Now, this statement can be modified. Perhaps what people really mean when they say it is, 'In optimal circumstances, with sensitive support and trust, the client *ultimately* knows best'. In other words, counselling can hold the person, help them to restore their natural equilibrium and contact their own resources, and gradually the client will once again know how to feel, what to think and do in order to best continue with his or her life in a healthier way. This acknowledges that *temporarily* the client *doesn't* know best. Isn't this a more realistic statement? But some might object that the client does always know best, but temporarily she has forgotten what she knows or has lost faith in her ability to know, or does in fact always know deep down what is best for her. A woman who is subjected to domestic violence but remains in the abusive situation apparently doesn't know best while she clings to the hope that her partner may change, and she still loves him. But deep down perhaps she knows what the odds are and also knows that this isn't yet quite the best time to leave.

Our original statement, 'The client knows best', may be simply a corrective to the dangerous assumption that the counsellor knows best. In some ways counselling was always a reaction against the view that the doctor or the psychiatrist knows best. Perhaps some ultra-loyal humanistic counsellors are responsible for propagating the myth that the client (always) knows best, as a corrective. It seems more likely, however, that some genuinely believe this view to be correct and not a myth.

It might be the case that neither the client nor the counsellor knows best. The client may be reeling from recent challenging life events and the counsellor is simply doing his fallible best at any one time. It might well be that at any given moment the client knows best whether the counsellor's utterances are accurate and empathic, or mistaken, wide of the mark. In this sense, it is true that the client knows best how she feels at any one moment. The client knows if the counsellor has hit the nail on the head with his last statement. But she may not know best what to do, or what is the best decision in the long run: 'Yes I know I feel extremely emotional about being pregnant but I don't know what to do for the best'. The client may decide (has to decide) in the immediate term what to do, but may later regret it.

We live with phrases like 'It's all for the best' and 'Everything has a reason' and mostly these are unexamined statements that may not stand up to close analysis. 'I did the best I could at the time', is a common enough statement of this kind, often supported by counsellors who believe in the 'organismic valuing process'. This tradition rests heavily on faith in emotion: 'It felt right at the time'. 'The client knows best' is a well-meaning statement of faith. It is probably not strictly true that the client (always or ultimately) *knows* best, since few of us are skilled reasoners. Most of us subjectively know what *feels* best, or least uncomfortable or most exciting or manageable, at any one time. Perhaps we will be shown decisively in the not too distant future that in the matter of evaluating and choosing optimally between all possible courses of action, based on all known and pertinent variables, it is the computer, and not the client or counsellor, that knows best!

Further reading

Anderson, H. & Goolishian, H. (1992) The client is the expert: a not-knowing approach to therapy. In S. McNamee & K.J. Gergen (eds), *Therapy as Social Construction*. London: Sage.

Must Counselling Embrace an Optimistic View of Human Nature and Potential?

Implicitly, all counselling rests on a belief that whatever it is that the client brings – however negative and distressing it is – something can be done about it. This doesn't mean that all counsellors think in terms of guaranteed improvements in clients' lives but it is always implied, I think, that counselling is at least worth a shot, and very likely to make a positive difference. Even if this difference isn't always quite what the client wants, the implication is a hopeful one: try counselling and something worthwhile is likely to happen. In this sense all counselling and all counsellors are optimistic. But things are more complicated than they might at first appear. Optimism varies enormously from one person to another, from culture to culture, era to era, and according to each theoretical model of counselling.

Consider first the individual counsellor. Must applicants for counselling training have optimistic personalities? Presumably no-one who comes across as deeply negative and depressed will be offered a place on a training course. But we can imagine a spectrum from extremely (perhaps Pollyanna-ishly) optimistic, through highly, fairly, not optimistic, to deeply pessimistic. Probably, only those on the more positive side of this spectrum are likely to be accepted on to a course. But isn't it a little more complicated? Perhaps it is possible to be a little pessimistic about oneself and/or the world and the future and yet be interpersonally warm and open towards other people. In other words, must the counsellor embody optimism in order to work effectively as a counsellor? It may be possible to bracket general views about human nature and potential while paying full, respectful attention to each client. It would not, however, be authentic to *feign* optimism while with clients. Equally, it is an unhelpful but not unheard of practice for some therapists to convey emphatic pessimism about certain conditions, as in, for example, 'Nothing can be done for anyone with severe OCD'.

Whatever your views about human nature, you might conceivably find reasons to be hopeful about the particularity of humanity in working with each client (or perhaps some clients more than others), while feeling pessimistic about politicians, say. And the obverse of all this is to ask about the limits of the suitability of counsellors with pathologically optimistic personalities. In other words, might there be some danger entailed in allowing people to become counsellors who have a surfeit of uncritically upbeat views about clients, society and life generally? One criticism of the self-help book market is that it thrives on optimistic messages – people buy into it and believe it precisely for this reason. We might also ask whether all the clinical psychological professions do not constitute a form of structured optimism.

Americans are usually seen, broadly speaking, as belonging to an optimistic, pragmatic, self-help, 'can-do' culture: obstacles can be overcome and perhaps the sky's the limit. The same would probably not be said of French, German or Finnish people, for example. Jewish culture is probably less optimistic (based on terrible Jewish suffering) than a Christian culture that is based on a belief in salvation. Counselling that takes place in a country that enjoys a high standard of living and realistic prospects for personal advancement is likely to differ from counselling within a country where high levels of poverty, hunger, disease and corruption predominate. Counselling during wartime will differ from counselling during a period of sustained peace.

It is a simple matter to observe that those models originating in and around wartime Europe, most of them associated with Jewish founders, are not highly optimistic. Those who emigrated to the UK and USA perhaps became a little less pessimistic. Founders of the humanistic approaches from around the 1950s, many of them living in or associated with the (sunny) west coast of the USA, are among the most optimistic. Psychoanalytic models are much more at home in east coast USA. The 1970s wave of 'extreme' therapies, such as re-evaluation co-counselling, primal therapy, rebirthing and transpersonal therapies, although imported in part to the UK, were perhaps tempered by the British attitude. Solution-focused therapy likewise, while getting a reasonable reception in the UK, has perhaps had less success than it might due to a poor fit with British dourness. On the other hand, cognitive behaviour therapy (CBT), also originating in the USA from a disillusionment with psychoanalytic practice, found a receptive audience in the UK. CBT is neither wildly optimistic nor pessimistic but seems pitched at a modest level of personal experimentation, hard work and reality-testing; it may also appeal to British stoicism.

At the level of in-session one-to-one counselling, a fair degree of realistic hope being conveyed to the client seems necessary in general, although in principle psychoanalytic and person-centred practitioners may not want to influence the client in any direction. It is commonly accepted that things may become more painful and difficult in counselling before they get better, so clients may need to tolerate at least some period of apparently lowered hope. But long-term, deep personal pessimism is associated with depression and most counsellors will probably be concerned about this. A too rapid or abrupt adoption of an over-optimistic attitude may often be taken to signify a 'flight into health' or even mania, however. Some will regard both optimism and pessimism (or hope and despair) as normal fluctuating moods, part of the healthy flow of anyone's experience.

Might we attempt to resolve this question at least partly by research measuring client views and outcomes against counsellors' and therapists' personalities?

Further reading

Weatherill, R. (2004) *Our Last Great Delusion: A Radical Psychoanalytical Critique of Therapy Culture*. Exeter: Imprint Academic.

Counselling Wisdom:

Challenge

Certain beliefs strongly permeate counselling, such as its alleged non-directiveness. Sometimes these become uncritical mantras, repeated so often that few will stop to reconsider their meaning. It can prove useful to question some of our most hallowed beliefs here, for example that the relationship is the be all and end all of successful counselling. Do you find yourself holding any of these views and perhaps repeating them without sufficient critical reflection? On the other hand, if certain pieces of wisdom do seem absolutely key to you, can you articulate why, and where the author is going wrong in critiquing them? Try to identify further pieces of practice wisdom and their basis in faith or evidence.

Case Study

During a personal development group Ian angrily explodes at Sheila, another student, telling her that he's sick of the way she trots out meaningless clichés and psychobabble. At first Sheila is taken aback and becomes defensive, and her peers come to her aid. But an interesting debate ensues about the ease and frequency with which certain terms are used, how vague, romantic and mesmerizing they can be and what they may conceal. Do you agree that this happens and is significant? Are the terms 'journey', 'process' and 'relationship', for example, in this category? Similarly, are assumptions about therapeutic optimism, client expertise and non-directiveness really valid? Is there a real body of counselling wisdom as opposed to a habit of uncritically repeating clichés? (See Rosen, 1977; Spurling, 1993.)

Critical thinking perspectives

Ian, Sheila and others might agree that they would like to explore as honestly as possible how they all really feel instead of portraying how they think they are supposed to feel and behave as counsellors. They could also agree to help each other expose the clichés and assumptions they habitually rely on. In order to do this they would have to suspend the anxieties that they or their facilitators had in relation to who is suitable to become a counsellor, so that the deepest, most idiosyncratic and potentially weird and objectionable aspects of themselves might emerge. Sheila might discover that beneath her habitual optimism sit defences that she is terrified to disturb; Ian might come to dislike his own pessimism and cynicism. This experiential critical thinking, observing and interaction would require a great deal of time and trust. Is this 'doable' when so many other, more 'substantive' topics have to be covered?

The Spectrum of
Suffering

Can Counselling or Psychotherapy Help people with Serious Mental Health Problems?

It used to be thought that almost any psychological problem could be addressed effectively by one form or another of talking therapy, and some practitioners still believe this to be the case. We are on contentious ground when we begin discussing schizophrenia, bipolar disorder, obsessive compulsive disorder (OCD), severe depression, autism and other stubborn conditions. Many humanistic therapists reject all such labelling and the psychiatric assumptions that accompany it. Some psychoanalytic therapists regard all such labels as symptoms of underlying unconscious conflicts. However, psychiatric wisdom in recent years has it that most of these are (as yet not fully understood) problems with genetic origins that are best managed pharmacologically. Clinical psychologists would also argue that some of them, such as OCD, are helped by CBT, often alongside medication.

It used to be believed that 'schizophrenogenic mothers' had a large part to play in the cause of schizophrenia and that deep talking therapy could make real inroads on the schizophrenia itself. I have indeed heard some psychodynamic counsellors claiming successes with OCD. At the other end of the spectrum, I have heard a pioneer of CBT claiming evangelically at a conference that only CBT can successfully address OCD and that claims to success by psychodynamic counselling and NLP are 'nonsense'. NICE guidelines tend to reinforce the view that combinations of certain medications and CBT-oriented therapies are the optimal treatments. Yet others consider that there is a very wide range of unique human experiences that get inappropriately assessed and diagnosed as hardened psychiatric categories. So clearly this is contentious territory.

Radical humanistic therapists seem to believe that – given optimal levels of respect, patience and therapeutic skill – people with 'severe mental health problems' (and even this term may be rejected) can be helped. Such help may lead towards a 'cure', or to comforting insights, self-acceptance, self-management strategies or simply a sense of human solidarity. It is also often asserted that 'schizophrenia' refers to a different kind of human experience, with internal voices deserving respect. There may well be some truth in these perspectives but dangers lie in inflating the therapeutic value of such approaches and undermining counterclaims. The admirable passion driving such attitudes may cloud reason and pragmatism; a client who is suffering acutely and may be a danger to himself or others may sometimes be better served by medication. Recalcitrant radicals in the counselling world are effective at drawing attention to possible abuses of highly distressed human beings, but a valid protest can become obstructive dogma. Occasionally, naïve counsellors seem to believe that they can effect a cure for a client's severe mental health condition, and this can lead to delayed effective help or an exacerbation of problems (for example, by probing and challenging too strenuously), and occasionally, of course, they may actually – probably fortuitously – prove very helpful.

It is usually agreed that one area in which counsellors and other talking therapists can be helpful is in providing support and hope. It may also be the case that the client needs to discuss an issue unrelated to the primary diagnostic problem. For example, anyone can experience an unexpected bereavement and look for help to work through its effects. People with autism are not usually 'cured' by counselling but often training in social skills can be helpful.

The rule of thumb here is to consider carefully whether to take on new clients with known severe mental health problems, especially when the counsellor is relatively inexperienced. Where it emerges during counselling that a client may have such a condition, careful discussion in supervision is called for. A decision may then follow to continue with the client or to refer them on. Given that many such problems have their onset at certain life stages (for instance, schizophrenia, bipolar disorder and OCD from adolescence, dementia from early old age), assessment should help to pick these up and refer on.

One does not have to be a diehard pro-psychiatric practitioner to have faith in medication, nor a radical anti-psychiatric practitioner to earn a reputation for valuing clients' rights. The optimal position is probably a readiness to balance clients' wishes and needs against current knowledge in the field, the available resources and approximate prognoses. Occasionally it may be acceptable cautiously to 'have a go' with a client when improvement is scented.

But over-ambitious and naïve tendencies when working with vulnerable and severely distressed clients should generally be avoided. On the other hand, you may ask what it is that makes one person (like me) sceptical about talking therapies for severe mental health problems, while another, perhaps in the Laingian tradition, is radically in favour of them.

Further reading

Bentall, R. (2009) *Doctoring the Mind: Why Psychiatric Treatment Fails*. London: Allen Lane.

Joseph, S. & Worsley, R. (eds) (2005) *Person-Centred Psychopathology: A Positive Psychology of Mental Health*. Ross-on-Wye: PCCS.

Kotowicz, Z. (1997) *R.D. Laing and the Paths of Anti-Psychiatry*. London: Routledge.

48

Are we all Neurotic?

The term 'neurotic' is not in favour today as much as it was three decades or so ago but still carries the meaning of psychological and behavioural oddness or a vulnerability to personal problems. We can look at this question from several angles. The simplest one is to say that the vast majority of human beings are stable, healthy, resilient and decent, and hence not neurotic. Conversely, we can say that a minority display signs of not being able to cope with life challenges, as being particularly prone to anxiety and depression and other mental health problems. In other words, there are two groups of people. But some would still insist that we are all deeply neurotic, that neurosis is a total neurophysiological state that no human being can escape in a damaged civilization. And some would also suggest that certain groups are neurotic, for example, those who are over-educated, city dwellers or Westerners.

This question is important for counselling. Counselling has always been based on a premise that almost anyone can benefit from it. Even if we do not have psychiatric symptoms or visibly debilitating problems, we may have worrying preoccupations or subclinical problems, or we may wish to improve aspects of our functioning. The grief of bereavement is not neurotic, the depression following redundancy isn't neurotic. But people do struggle with such experiences. Opponents of a 'counselling for all' approach argue that we have always coped with normal upsets and that counselling undermines our natural ability to cope and merely panders to the 'worried well'.

However, let's remember the much-promoted figure that one in four of us in the UK will experience a mental health problem in our lifetime and one in four in the USA (NIMH, 2009). It's clear that depression is very common, not only in the UK but also worldwide, and figures are given for various conditions, for example 1 per cent of the population suffer from schizophrenia, 2 per cent have OCD, up to 15 per cent may have psychopathic traits, and so on. It's not my intention here to trace sources and analyse errors and reasons but to bring out two issues: first, that mental health problems of various degrees of severity are probably very common, and second, that there is a great deal of dispute surrounding such claims. My approach is to ask what we mean by neurosis or mental health problems.

One retort is to ask: 'Neurotic compared with what or whom?' Are human beings neurotic compared with animals or modern human beings neurotic compared with how we imagine them to have been some time ago? We are told that some animals can display neurotic symptoms, particularly those in zoos or other crowded conditions. We can point to people who clearly have severe problems like schizophrenia or psychopathic personality disorders, including long-term hospitalized people and violent criminals, and declare that the vast majority of us are not like that. Indeed 'neurotic' used to be contrasted with 'psychotic'.

A huge problem facing us when we ask such questions is that people may conceal how they actually feel or what is going on in their private lives. While some of us may want to declare ourselves neurotic, or cannot deny it, others find such terms stigmatic, or pride may prevent them from admitting to any 'weakness'. Since we have no consensus about what constitutes a neurosis or mental health problem, we cannot appeal to an objective criterion. Questionnaires abound which can ostensibly do just this but they may only crudely capture obvious and moderate-to-severe conditions.

I have argued elsewhere in this book that human beings suffer from 'anthropathology' – a sickness of human beings. Obviously many disagree with this view and may even find it ridiculous. A lot depends on the terms we are using. We can argue that there is a great deal wrong with the human species, that we all suffer from some psychological and moral flaw that affects our personal feelings, thoughts and behaviour but also our collective lifestyles and our social structures. Some would agree that capitalist greed, dishonesty, war and other phenomena are symptoms of human neurosis. Freud argued that the necessity of suppressing our deepest animal desires may lead to a collective neurosis and many Jungians also demonstrate such connections. By this reasoning, we are all indeed self-evidently neurotic, and if this is so then it is hardly surprising that some of us manifest even more grave symptoms than the rest, and thus may bear the stigma of madness that somehow makes the rest of us feel that we're not so badly off.

Now, if we are *all* neurotic, then this includes counsellors, therapists and psychologists – the very people assigned to help us overcome our problems and neuroses. In a sense this is acknowledged by the requirement that therapists have their own therapy but even this is no guarantee of their freedom from neurosis or mild mental health problems. Put differently, if neurosis is something like a subtle systemic trait in individuals and society (as I believe it is, if we agree to disagree on terminology) then many will not want or be able to recognize it. 'Neurotic' is indeed an unhelpfully vague term, as perhaps 'anthropathology' also is. Overlaps between psychiatric, psychological and moral categories also cloud the issue. I would like to be able to appeal to intuition – don't we all just *know* that we're neurotic? Or don't those among us who are really honest know? Unfortunately this won't work. But neither will any appeal to semantics or psychometrics, since those who drive such disciplines tend to immerse themselves in neurotic detail, at least in my view.

Further reading

Wood, G. (1984) *The Myth of Neurosis: A Case for Moral Therapy*. London: Macmillan.
Young, S.F. (1991) *I'm Not OK and You're Not OK Either*. London: Bloomsbury.

49

Are there Limits to Personal Change in Counselling?

CBT tends to have fairly realistic, well-defined goals, and psychodynamic models also tend to have somewhat circumscribed aims. Humanistic approaches, however, particularly those aligned with 'human potential', often have grander aspirations. The counselling movement generally – with its emphasis on increasing the client's resourcefulness and capacity for positive problem solving, and sometimes using phrases such as 'the fully functioning person' – perhaps invites almost unlimited aspirations and fantasies. In parallel with media portrayals of the cosmetic 'make-over', some people have come to believe that talking therapies and coaching might be used to radically change their personality, mend their marriage or cut short their grief. Some therapies (such as primal) have promised '*the* cure for neurosis', access to higher levels of consciousness and so on.

Consider the range of what clients can bring to counselling:

'I want to be able to fancy my wife again and enjoy the kind of wild sex with her that we used to have'.
'I want to lose my shyness and be able to talk confidently with anyone'.
'I want to become a successful entrepreneur like the people on The Apprentice'.
'I want to put my sexual abuse and all my other baggage behind me once and for all'.
'I want to be a successful writer'.

Complications along these lines might include an older client saying she wants to get her youthful energy back; an autistic person wanting a cure for their autism; someone with a history of depression wanting to become a very upbeat, optimistic person; a gay man wanting to become heterosexual; and so on. I am not saying that all such examples are out of the question. It may be that some inroads can be made on many of these concerns. It is certainly the case that some therapists claim solutions due to their own grandiosity or evangelical beliefs, and sometimes unscrupulously. Of course, it's always possible too that occasionally a client may make an unpredictable, apparently miraculous turn-around. But generally there are probable limits for most of these scenarios.

It is certainly true that we cannot always know what anyone's potential is. Well-meaning counsellors will often want to work hard and take their best shot at seeing whether they can help a client where no previous efforts have worked successfully. There are some documented cases of dramatic breakthroughs but also reasons to believe that at least some of these may be exaggerated or not durable.

'It's never too late,' and 'You can always change the way you are' are popular optimistic statements. But it may be that for most of us, particularly as we get older, habits are reinforced, opportunities are more limited, energy is lower and radical change is much harder than ever. It *is* too late in your fifties, for example, to train to become a ballet dancer or professional footballer. It is sometimes unwise to try too hard, too abruptly, to take on something too new, for instance to launch into a vigorous exercise programme in your fifties from a position of nil exercise, thus inviting a heart attack.

A caveat about CBT's realistic scope may be seen in the very title of one of Albert Ellis's books on rational emotive behaviour therapy – *How to Stubbornly Refuse to Make Yourself Miserable about Anything – Yes Anything!* This does seem to be claiming too much and could belong in the slightly dangerous territory of leaving clients feeling inadequate or guilty if they cannot meet such claims. Also, I am not suggesting that most humanistic counsellors are unethically giving hope for miraculous changes that are unlikely to occur. But some do, particularly in private practice; indeed this entire question may be constellated in terms of the integrity of the private practitioner since practitioners working in other settings are likely to face assessment protocols, waiting lists and time constraints. The optimal position is probably to be honest with clients, to be willing to 'have a go' where it seems reasonable, and overall to help clients accept themselves no matter what. The ambitious humanistic therapist who really does believe sincerely in the possibilities for radical or dramatic change should at least make clients aware that his or her approach is not guaranteed to deliver everything that is wished for.

Further reading

Ferrucci, P. (1990) *Inevitable Grace: Breakthroughs in Self-Realization*. Wellingborough: Aquarian.

Sandler, J. & Dreher, A.U. (1996) *What Do Psychoanalysts Want? The Problem of Aims in Psychoanalysis*. London: Routledge.

50

Which Undiscovered Diagnostic Categories Might There Be?

By undiscovered diagnostic categories (UDCs) I mean presenting problems or disorders that can be recognized but are either not yet very common or not labelled. If you dislike or refute the very idea of diagnostic categories, it may help to think in terms of tendencies and clusters of behaviours. It can also be helpful to consider that clinical terminology changes and that the 300+ listed disorders in the *DSM* themselves change somewhat every few years. It may even be the case that these appear or increase in relation to social changes or fashions, or incipient neurotic epidemics. In recent times there have been speculations about so-called road rage and desk rage. Some are talking about orthorexia and athletica nervosa, conditions entailing an exaggerated and unhealthy concern with correct, acceptable food, and fitness and body image respectively. It is certainly the case that 'comorbidity' is a common phenomenon, that is, the co-existence of two or more recognizable clinical conditions or therapeutic concerns. Here are three suggestive examples.

Dystechnia – I use this putative term instead of technophobia. Discussion of technophobia (a word not in use more than 10 to 20 years ago) tends towards the view that people have some degree of learning difficulty and refuse to engage in the learning necessary for conquering anxieties about technology, computers in particular. I have found (as a so-called 'technophobe') that sufferers are often met with jokes and rebuttals. In other words, you don't really have a problem, you're putting it on or exaggerating it, or are just plain lazy. Not so long ago those who struggled to read and write or process information were called illiterate or regarded as malingerers. Now dyslexia is taken very seriously. My guess – as someone who struggles with technology and gets anxious and depressed in relation to it – is that it will one day be recognized as a quite stubborn condition related to subtle personality factors including difficulty in coping with complex sequences. I have not found that it responds to behavioural training or CBT-like interventions.

Dysmorphophobia of the other (DOTO) – This is obviously an extension of the principle of body dysmorphic disorder but whereas that condition is about people finding themselves exaggeratedly ugly and physically unacceptable, DOTO is about finding others ugly or unacceptable. On the face of it, this might sound more like a repellent personality trait than a distressing and 'treatable' condition. Its most obvious arena is in couple formation and maintenance, in other words in how we come to be and remain attracted to romantic partners. As one extreme view, there are those who insist that 'looks (and other sensory attributes) are altogether unimportant' or secondary to personality characteristics. But a moment's reflection shows how common and stubborn this tendency is. Most women strongly prefer taller men, for example, and many men prefer younger women. Some are attracted to or repelled by specific features such as eye or hair colour, slimness, buttocks, breasts, hands, youthfulness, as well as voice, accent, gait and so on. Smell, or olfactory and pheromonal properties, can also be a subtle attractor or repellent. Someone who suffers from DOTO either cannot get close to another who possesses such idiosyncratically sensed undesirable features, or cannot persist with a relationship when they become apparent. Also, illness, surgery and ageing can of course trigger significant bodily changes that not all partners can accept.

The point about DOTO is that it can easily be dismissed or misdiagnosed as a neurotic or immature characteristic (perhaps belonging more to men than women) and can also be addressed by inappropriate therapy. DOTO may be a kind of aversive or obsessive disorder with little or no root in childhood experience; rather, it may have genetic origins and may not respond to talking therapy. Years of individual and couple counselling might be wasted searching for non-existent 'psychodynamic' causes. It may be helpful to think of it in terms of a deeply-rooted perfectionism or phobia.

Post-ecstatic intrusive thoughts (PEIT) – We now accept the term and the condition of PTSD, post-traumatic stress disorder, which is characterized by involuntary, intrusive thoughts and flashbacks of unpleasant or horrific experiences. But some of us experience powerful thoughts and images that are connected with extreme pleasure and that we cannot shake off, however dysfunctional they are. Drug addiction and extreme sexual pleasure are primary examples. Other examples might include spiritual and extreme sports experiences. Anyone who has experienced such highs in the past and cannot command their return will understand the pain and anguish that may be involved. If afflicted by sports injuries and unable to play again, the sportsman may feel bereft and unable to cope without excessive alcohol, for example. You may feel devastated to realize that your best sexual, artistic or other pleasures are behind you, or at least you may believe this to be the case. Such preoccupations can prevent you from getting on with life. They may resemble bereavement and may or may not respond to counselling of one kind or another.

In refusing to consider that there may be unrecognized or emerging 'disorders' of these kinds, we may fail as counsellors to be duly empathic and to offer an appropriate therapy. We may become judgemental (dystechnia is laziness, DOTO is sexist or ageist, PEIT is merely an addiction and an excuse for not growing up) and not take them seriously enough. We may not get engaged in the necessary research. But it is also a creative exercise to reflect on clients' and our own idiosyncratic experiences and to consider whether a shared problem may exist that has not yet been named. Equally, those opposed to all 'labelling' can either dismiss such ideas altogether or ask themselves what their precise objections and alternative strategies are. Perhaps we do already have far too many listed disorders. How should we construct a debate around these topics?

Further reading

Kutchins, H. & Kirk, S.A. (1997) *Making Us Crazy: DSM – The Psychiatric Bible and the Creation of Mental Disorders*. London: Constable.

Is the Human Species
Anthropathological?

I need to explain immediately what this means and how it is relevant to counselling. Anthropathology refers to 'the sickness of humankind'. It draws together all our dysfunctional traits at a macro-level and argues that these pervade our lives both individually and collectively. At our visible worst, we are selfish, war-mongering, greedy, deceptive, environmentally destructive and seemingly incapable of learning from our past mistakes. At collective and individual levels we are addicted to many counter-productive traditions and habits. Vast inequalities in wealth distribution reflect our greed, rationalized in capitalism. Lies are structurally necessary in a capitalist society (for example, in sales, advertising, public relations) and also in everyday interpersonal relations. Arguably our major institutions are not fit for purpose: education fails to prepare us for sane, constructive adult life, work is often soul-destroying, marriage often breaks down. The course of each human life is marked by a relatively early peak of energy and health, followed by a gradual decline into old age and death. This is not to overlook traits of goodness in human beings and the pleasures to be found in life but to point out the daunting obstacles.

Now, the relevance of this view for counselling is as follows. We often assume that individual problems in living are 'vertical' in kind, that is, caused by early life experiences, and by what goes on in our heads. We pay lip service to the inclusion of social contexts material in training. But we don't usually consider that everyday life is 'neurotogenic', in other words that the very milieu in which we live – stressful jobs, a busy family life, financial insecurity, bureaucratic demands and so on – damages our wellbeing and undermines the gains made by counselling. These are 'horizontal' pressures that are marginalized in counselling theory. Our professional bodies are themselves riven by social expectations and compromises. In other words, ours is a 'mad world' that doesn't ultimately have to be this way, that makes us ill, and yet we cannot escape from it or change it significantly. If there is any truth in this account, then it also follows that our usual theories about what causes psychological dysfunction may be highly inaccurate or inadequate. And we may be unintentionally encouraging our clients to change their feelings and thoughts instead of agitating for a different kind of society.

I believe that this account *is* largely accurate, yet I am aware that it isn't widely accepted. It is also true that it must be associated with pessimism and an agenda for change that is probably macro-level and long-term at best. Counsellors are fairly optimistic, they are concerned with the person suffering in front of them, with proximal phenomena. Each client is probably a recipient of a complex blend of evolutionary and genetic factors on the one hand, and layers of socio-economic and cultural damage on the other. But she or he has to be addressed as (or 'as if'?) a relatively free agent living fully in the here and now.

The other side of this coin too is that the counsellor presumably believes that she herself is an effective agent for change. We do not generally see ourselves as highly damaged and as unable to do much about it. But we are enmeshed in the same systemic problems as others, having to earn a livelihood, maintain a relationship and house, suffering from health problems and ageing. We *may* be relatively more resourceful or insightful than our clients. But all of us face macro-economic vicissitudes, environmental threats, the possibility of war and so on. Your client may be made redundant and wants to talk through the problems involved, but you too, as an employed counsellor, may face work stress, a high caseload and the possibility of redundancy.

All the above may not initially seem like a species problem; it could be regarded as a set of transient cultural challenges. Yet it does look as if such problems will always be with us. Counselling may help to take the edge off some of the passing crises from which we can all suffer but it does not have the potency to make necessary, radical social changes. Anthropathology brings up questions about genetic propensities to various kinds of suffering: sometimes we will be better off tracing genetic causes and making due adaptations. Anthropathology also asks questions about our patriarchal society, which probably underpins wars and entails subtle phenomena like the suppression of tenderness. We can encourage or facilitate tenderness and catharsis in counselling as much as we like but our clients remain in an emotion-suppressing patriarchal macro-culture.

It is arguably the enormity, pervasiveness and persistence of anthropathology that prevent us from making any meaningful impression on our culture, in spite of a well-meaning but naïve discourse about emotional intelligence. But there are strong arguments against such essentialist ideas too.

Further reading

Feltham, C. (2007) *What's Wrong with Us? The Anthropathology Thesis*. Chichester: Wiley.

Fromm, E. (1963) *The Sane Society*. London: Routledge & Kegan Paul.

The Spectrum of Suffering:

Perhaps there are broadly two opposed camps on the question of suffering. On the one hand, many dislike the very vocabulary of neurosis, psychopathology, psychiatric disorders or even problems. On the other, some believe that counselling is weak and naïve in the face of massive human suffering. Where do you place yourself on these positions? Arguably, it matters a great deal and has a lot to say about how counselling is constructed and how it is presented to potential clients. It also fundamentally affects how we see ourselves. Are you, is the author, neurotic? If so, what are the limits of counselling in rooting out or modifying these negative traits? Are the identified issues brought by clients circumscribed or merely the tip of an impossibly large iceberg of human suffering?

Steven is a young man suffering from OCD, social isolation and depression. CBT has not helped him but medication has improved his mood. Assessments have considered whether a social phobia or Asperger's Syndrome may be part of his problems. The Japanese term *hikikomori* might also apply if he lived in that culture. Clinical literature says that OCD is not fully understood, that it seems to have genetic origins and perhaps 'epigenetic' features, but overall the prognosis is frequently quite negative. Steven's life is at standstill. An acquaintance suggests body psychotherapy. Steven himself is a vegan, very intelligent, and depressed by the state of the world and his poor job prospects. How would you counsel him? Is he simply suffering more acutely than some, while living in a 'mad world' and surrounded by professionals with no real answers? Are there sometimes no answers but only endurance? (See Charlton, 2000; Sanders, 2005.)

Critical thinking perspectives

A radical person-centred approach might regard Steven as simply a unique individual requiring intensive therapy from a practitioner loyal to person-centred principles; given time, he will come to accept himself and grow strong enough to find his own way. Indeed time with no therapy may lead to an improvement. One perspective on cases like Steven's suggests that the field of therapy is highly hit or miss, characterized by dozens of clinical opinions but no consensus or precision. From an anthropathological perspective we are all suffering, even if in slightly different ways and often to varying degrees. Yet the therapy world finds it impossible to accept a tragic view – that some forms of suffering may be simply incurable, that we do not really know specific causes or effective remedies for many individuals' ills. Then again, it could be that genetic and medical research might yet discover the causes of OCD and linked treatments. Why does the field seem to be riven by opposing theoretical camps? Why are we so wedded to traditions rather than passionate about discovery?

Perennial and Current Topics

52

How much Depends on the Client?

Almost all counselling theory is predicated on the principle that counsellors skilfully facilitate change. If you have the right kind of training and can learn the appropriate attitudes, skills and techniques, success should follow. When it doesn't, or when there seem to be glitches, the counsellor may consider if this was an appropriate referral or if she or he needs to try a different tack. Counsellors, particularly beginners, will sometimes berate themselves for not being able to get the client to return from small talk or circularity to a serious commitment to explore and change. But very often there will be some discussion in supervision about the client's resistance, reluctance, lack of psychological-mindedness or motivation, about his not being ready for change or in the 'precontemplative' stage. It's not exactly blaming the client but this is an area of acknowledged difficulty.

Some counsellors will respond to this scenario by honouring the client's stuckness, that is, by accepting that the client feels unable to move forward right now. Pain may be anticipated and the client may understandably hesitate or freeze. If the client needs to spend several sessions apparently meandering purposelessly, then that is his right and need. Patience may be rewarded. Or a point may come when the counsellor congruently discloses her or his discomfort and then the client may 'perk up' and respond to this challenge. Sometimes, probably, clients simply do not know how to use counselling optimally. Explanations about counselling and re-contracting may help to re-start the process.

Some research suggests that often clients will have done some preliminary work on their problems and will then seek counselling when they can't make further progress alone. The steps involved in finding and contacting a counsellor can be psychologically taxing for many. A client has to some extent to lay himself open to a complete stranger, to disclose what is frequently embarrassing, confusing and painful. He has to sense whether this is a counsellor he can trust, someone who can genuinely tune in, engage and have something to offer. He has to talk, process the emotions aroused, correct the counsellor when necessary, agree to and undertake homework if set and keep coming back week after week. He has to maintain hope when depression or despair weigh on him, and probably he has to do all this while also maintaining a job, relationships and family life. The counsellor will usually spend one hour with him, perhaps also think about him and talk about him sometimes in supervision. But the main bulk of the work lies with the client.

The counsellor has some sense of a typical temporal process in counselling and can mentally compare different clients and their issues and successes. The client has none of this background but must weigh up what benefits are or are not accumulating in this strange endeavour. It is not only courage in facing up to his problems that is required but an assessment of the pros and cons. Is the pain worth it? Is it worth the money and/or time and effort? How much risk is involved? Is he being understood more than misunderstood? What overall impact is the process going to have on his everyday life, his job and family, as well as internally, psychically?

We may easily forget that while counsellors have freely and fully opted into the culture of counselling (its sometimes 'heroic' emotional and behavioural requirements, technical language and so on), clients will naturally vary in their level of investment. A huge amount depends on clients as a whole but each client will bring something very different and the outcomes will probably differ enormously. The passionate commitment and expectation of many beginning counsellors are sometimes disappointed on finding that these are not matched by all clients. This is not to demean clients in any way but to recognize realistically the sheer diversity of the levels of commitment involved.

Counselling cannot progress without a client's co-operation, however true it is that some of this depends on the counsellor's skill in eliciting trust and effort, in helping the client to surrender his defences, to express necessary emotion and take therapeutic risks. Counsellors must be acutely aware of the common sensitivity displayed by clients (by any of us) when challenged. And clients must realize (must be helped to realize) that some challenge and discomfort have to be tolerated and learned from. Unfortunately those who are highly fragile, unless handled with great care, are most likely to withdraw from counselling if they feel too much discomfort at any one time. Those with good ego strength, good social support and resources may be most likely to benefit from counselling.

The subtleties involved in the client's personality and decision to have counselling, his view of the relationship with his counsellor, his immersion in the ongoing process, alongside the inevitable unvoiced calculations as to the risks and chances of success, are complex enough. But all these interact with the subtleties of the counsellor's personality, perceptiveness and skill.

Further reading

Duncan, B.L., Miller, S.D. & Sparks, J.A. (2004) *The Heroic Client: A Revolutionary Way to Improve Effectiveness through Client-Directed, Outcome-Informed Therapy*. San Francisco, CA: Jossey-Bass.

Fernandes, F. (2008) Working with the concept of stuckness. In W. Dryden (ed.), *Key Issues for Counselling in Action* (2nd edn). London: Sage.

Is Counselling Primarily a Heartfelt Activity?

A word like 'heartfelt' may seem out of place in a text on counselling and probably isn't found in many texts. Yet consider alongside it terms such as 'love', 'intuition', 'compassion', 'caring', 'feeling', 'tenderness'. Sometimes these terms are used, but not often. I suspect there is something highly contentious at the heart of this question. As counselling has aspired to a professional status, its theories and curricula being strategically pumped up in the meantime, perhaps anything that smacks of simplicity, of counselling being fundamentally like a deep friendship rather than a complex professional skill set and academic subject, is suppressed or minimized.

Something possibly even harder to argue is that counselling, like nursing, is essentially a female-oriented activity. When we talk about object relations, maternal reverie, empathy and nurture, we are acknowledging a primary female influence on child development and associations with an intuitive understanding of the subtleties of emotion and the ability to be warmly communicative. What makes this hard to argue is that it risks a sexist stereotyping of women as emotional, and perhaps as over-emotional and under-intellectual; the corollary is that men are perceived as uncaring and lacking in emotional intelligence. Some may readily agree with this but it tends to offend 'politically correct' sensitivities. However let's look at the flip side of all this.

Is it true that some are more naturally intuitive and emotionally responsive than others? If so, is it true that these qualities are crucial for successful counselling (or for certain kinds of counselling)? I believe the answer to both of these is 'Yes'. Not all women are naturally intuitive in a counselling-oriented way, nor do all men lack this quality. Also, training may improve intuition and its related qualities, but training probably has limits. Another related question is about the extent to which counselling requires a balance of emotional and analytical skills. Again, questions of gender and stereotypes arise. Could it be that women tend to opt more for psychodynamic and humanistic approaches than for CBT-oriented approaches? Feminist therapies make it look this way. Also (as is suggested elsewhere in this book) most counselling theory is generated by men and the cognitive is in the ascendant. Additionally, notions of intuition are subtly downplayed within academia; in other words, there is a prejudice against raw emotion and direct knowledge, and a demand for theoretical justification. Crying remains an uncomfortable phenomenon and is rare in public and in educational institutions, as is expressed anger. Direct, heartfelt responses to the common human experiences of loss and heartache receive relatively little attention in counselling training.

Genuine, deep feeling and compassion transmit themselves non-verbally. The client is likely to know the difference between a counsellor who really cares deeply and one who either struggles to do so or who is primarily cognitively rather than emotionally oriented. Also, the 'feeling counsellor' may be more likely to 'see into the heart' of the client, as well as picking up defences against feeling in the client. This may lead to the client feeling safer or more challenged. Overall, it could certainly lead to a deeper level of work.

Maternal intuition is a necessary and powerful ingredient of human survival. Babies experience bodily needs and discomforts, and can cry deeply (communicate viscerally and urgently), before they learn any verbal language. Even adults, often at a subliminal level, tune into others in the visual, aural and olfactory domains before the verbal and semantic. Intimate human relations are based on gut-level and pre-theoretical knowledge. This knowledge is sometimes incorrect but sometimes a better guide than the analytical and ponderous.

Training for drama involves a high degree of immersion in and a respect for emotions. In order to get inside another's skin and act as if you are that person (a lot like empathy) you have to experience a range of feelings at some depth. Theory is insufficient. It is true that counselling training contains a mixture of theory, skills and experiential self-awareness components, but it may still be that the theoretical is privileged (especially in a formal educational setting) and the experiential or emotional may not be as deep and raw as it could be. While exercises in accessing and exploring emotions can be set up, there is some artificiality in these and perhaps it remains a puzzle how best to focus on, deepen and utilize the counsellor's feelings, although some attempts have been made to teach compassion.

Heartfelt sentiments towards others and emotional communication are necessary and important, and probably neglected and misunderstood. On the other hand, there are risks of sentimentality, of becoming over-emotional, and of mistaking woolly, emotional hunches for accurate intuition. There is some risk of aiming for a cathartic emotional release in the uncritical belief that feelings are everything. (See Furedi (2004) on 'the culture of emotionalism'.) Emotion can also be elevated into something pseudo-spiritual, a kind of false rendition of true feelings. But feeling moved or touched by another's pain is quite common and genuine, and yet can become a problem for counsellors who feel self-conscious about it, as if it might be unprofessional. It is curious that we have developed a culture (in counselling training as well as in society generally) that is suspicious of the rawness and simplicity of feelings. It is interesting to note that critical thinking has some respectability but that we have no comparable term for the heartfelt or emotional. Critical feelings? Critical affect? It doesn't quite work. In some ways this crucial emotional aspect of counselling does not sit well with the analytical and academic.

Further reading

Curtis, R., Matise, M. & Glass, M.S. (2003) Counselling students' views and concerns about weeping with clients: a pilot study. *Counselling and Psychotherapy Research,* 3 (4), 300–306.

Gilbert, P. (2005) *Compassion: Conceptualisations, Research and Use in Psychotherapy.* London: Routledge.

Is Counselling Scientific?

Probably for the most part counsellors and therapists would not claim that their work is scientific and would not aspire to have counselling considered a science. Indeed, historically counsellors have largely shunned the biomedical model associated with psychiatry in favour of a humanistic model that fully honours subjectivity. However, some psychoanalysts and psychotherapists have made scientific claims, in the sense of psychotherapy having neurological correlates and predictable features. Also, where psychologists do psychotherapy and counselling under the banners of clinical psychology and counselling psychology, they inevitably imply that the behavioural and cognitive science underpinning psychology informs the talking therapies. Another way in which counselling might be considered scientific is in being aligned with health sciences and a research methodology that has scientific features (such as that which finds its way into NICE guidelines).

What are we to make of this seeming confusion of identities? Presumably the talking therapies cannot claim to be scientific in the same sense as physics and biology are scientific. We see no formation of indisputable laws and predictable experimental outcomes in counselling, for example. Nothing in psychotherapy can compare to the laws of physics or the genome project. No psychotherapeutic procedure seems to have quite as predictable an impact as many medical procedures. Is counselling to be considered part of the social sciences (which by some accounts include anthropology, economics, education, geography, history, law, politics, psychology and sociology)? Two problems arise here: (1) there is a longstanding debate about whether most of these can themselves be regarded as properly scientific; and (2) many would place at least some of these disciplines in the arts and humanities group. Another, and more grave, problem for counselling as scientific is that it is sometimes negatively linked with what many scientists regard as pseudoscience (e.g. homeopathy and other complementary therapies). Recently some CAM (complementary and alternative medicine) degrees have been abolished in some universities (or from their science departments) for just such reasons.

For counselling to allow itself to move under the aegis of the Health Professions Council (HPC) or the Department of Health, or for it to appear within NICE guidelines, presumably it has to have some scientific credibility. Let us note that, somewhat strangely, the HPC contains art therapy and speech therapy among others – professions that surely cannot claim to be entirely scientific. For counselling to warrant funding within the NHS, presumably it has to bow to attempts to research it in classically medical terms, that is, in controlled trials comparing the effectiveness of (different models of) counselling against medications, waiting list only, CBT and other treatments and control groups. As many counsellors have pointed out, this view is based on a misunderstanding of counselling and is bound to lead to methodological problems. The manualizable therapies like CBT can be measured in a way that humanistic therapies cannot, for example. Some psychoanalysts have rejected the attempted alignment of their practice with health sciences, seeing it instead as a distinctive activity addressing individual human beings, with each case and outcome being unique.

In what sense might we claim that counselling is at all scientific? Are its methods and aims capable of being formulated as clear hypotheses, as valid, reliable, generalizable, falsifiable? We certainly cannot say with any confidence that method A, applied to psychological condition B for C weeks or months with client personality D, will lead to outcome F. It seems that CBT is able to declare that in a large proportion of cases clients with depression will reach a state of reduced depression and should remain relatively free of depression. But even here there are so many variables that a huge amount of follow-up corroborative research is necessary. Clearly a central problem is the uniqueness of each individual and the other variables always involved: the diagnostic clarity, personality features, complicating factors (including comorbidity), severity and variations in timing, therapist, etc.

Some therapists have at various times been hopeful of gaining scientific status but it may be a doomed project. So if counselling isn't scientific, what are the implications? The NHS currently funds chaplains to offer spiritual or pastoral support (and indeed there are efforts to investigate the 'scientific' properties of religious belief and prayer), and homeopathy, acupuncture and reflexology are also found in the NHS. Is there any problem in counselling being considered or classified as a complementary treatment or supportive service? It seems there is. Practitioners in private practice currently need only the interest and co-operation of individual clients to thrive, but those in health settings – or in any setting where a system of accountability cites scientific method, evidence or status as ingredients – need greater clarity. You must either demonstrate in what ways counselling meets scientific criteria, or provide an alternative justification for its funding and use. Actually, there is probably little rigorous evidence (or very mixed evidence) that education 'works', or indeed that economics or politics are sciences – yet they persist. And arguably psychology, for all its scientific aspiration and history, has produced little in the way of big breakthroughs or anything to compare with advances in hard medical knowledge.

Further reading

Hansen, J.T. (2005) The devaluation of inner subjective experience by the counseling profession: A plea to reclaim the essence of the profession. *Journal of Counseling and Development,* 50, 154–160.
Langs, R. (1999) *Psychotherapy and Science.* London: Sage.
Lilienfeld, S.O., Lynn, S.J. & Lohr, J.M. (eds) (2003) *Science and Pseudoscience in Clinical Psychology.* New York: Guilford.

55

What to Think about Suicide?

It's fairly well understood and accepted that counsellors and therapists must take seriously any hint of suicidal ideation or intention expressed by clients.

This is distinct from the sad but unactivated 'I wish I was dead' phrase that many of us have uttered at difficult times in our lives. The well-known rule of thumb is that clients should be sensitively asked if they have thought about actual plans and, following this, the counsellor should set in motion anti-suicide strategies with the client's co-operation. If necessary, counsellors may have to 'breach' confidentiality in order to speak to relevant professionals. But it is also acknowledged that practitioners in the NHS or other statutory services face different ethical responsibilities from those in private practice. Furthermore, it is evident that practitioners in different models may think differently about suicide – it may be regarded as a client's ultimate right, as a manifestation of certain defence mechanisms, or as an extreme example of irrational, depressed thinking.

However, the recent high profile given to assisted dying throws up many new challenges for counsellors. A steady trickle of cases has been publicized of relatives accompanying loved ones to the Dignitas Clinic in Zurich. Here, as in Oregon, Belgium, Holland and a tiny number of other states and countries, the practice of assisted dying is legal, unlike in the UK. Most of these cases involve older or elderly people with terminal or very serious illnesses but a few have been very contentious, involving serious disabilities at a younger age. Although people in these situations are carefully screened according to medical criteria, and offered counselling, many ethical and religious objections have been made. This growing phenomenon is included here because it *is* increasing in incidence, and looks like continuing to increase as the population ages. It is sure to find its way into mainstream counselling as such individuals or those close to them wrestle with their own views and intentions. This change of ethical culture has to be engaged with. Many with religious commitments are either opposed on principle or find themselves agonizing over the new challenges. Some counsellors too may feel compromised and seek guidance.

Let's consider two extreme views on this. First, there is the position that life is precious or sacred, and must be preserved at all costs. Reinforcing this view is the argument that counselling can address a loss of morale or depression, medical advances can assist palliatively, and nursing services and aids can bring comfort to people who are suffering physically. An even stronger view is that we have a duty to continue living against all odds. Indeed, ever increasing longevity seems to create an expectation that we must live long lives and perhaps we have internalized the idea that dying before the average life expectancy is something of a failure. To live the longest possible life, in this view, seems even more important than quality of life.

The second, opposite view is as follows. Life can be very difficult and painful but there is no God or higher locus of accountability. It is always *my* life or *your* life and each individual's rational decision is her or his own to make. When, for whatever reason, any one of us decides that life contains more pain than pleasure, more indignity than dignity, with little prospect of relief or improvement, it seems natural to consider suicide, or the termination of suffering. The principle in counselling that promotes the self-determination of the client tends often to uncritically support the belief that solutions always exist and courage can (and should) always be found. But some writers have pointed, for example, to a valid 'anti-heroic cancer narrative' (Diedrich, 2005), that is, that some of us simply cannot find courage or meaning within great suffering. Some of us may prefer death to protracted painful treatments like chemotherapy. Some will prefer not to extend their lives in severe physical or mental disability or pain.

In the latter scenario, where counsellors are involved they will naturally, sensitively and non-directively listen to clients' words and feelings, and the impact of any suicide or refusal of life-extending treatment on loved ones may well feature in sessions. Why should clients not rationally or even emotionally choose suicide when it is their preferred option? Wouldn't such dilemmas be better to be aired openly, and even suicide itself facilitated safely by the state in the UK, rather than being a desperate, furtive matter? Where counsellors hold religious or other views that are rigidly anti-suicidal there is an onus on them to reflect on these and make them known.

It is well known that the prominent psychotherapist Petruska Clarkson took her own life in 2006 and her suicide note mentioned the significance of the right to decide when one should die. This is not merely an academic matter. It affects us all and it behoves counsellors to consider carefully their own views so that they do not unthinkingly prevent or encourage suicide, but have the courage and wisdom to accompany clients facing such decisions to the emotional and rational depths necessary. I once asked a class of counselling students how many of them had ever considered suicide and most said they had at some stage. But the possible suicide of a client is also one of the most fraught with anxiety for students and practitioners.

To project the question of suicide somewhat into the future, some climate change scientists already predict worst case scenarios of uninhabitably hot countries, famines and resource wars. In such a world, possibly mere decades away, if counsellors were still to exist they might face much more frequent disclosures of rational suicidal ideation.

Further reading

Firestone, R.W. (1997) *Suicide and the Inner Voice: Risk Assessment, Treatment, and Case Management.* Thousand Oaks, CA: Sage.
Minois, G. (1999) *History of Suicide: Voluntary Death in Western Culture.* Baltimore, MD: Johns Hopkins University Press.
Paulson, B.L. & Worth, M. (2002) Counseling for suicide: client perspectives. *Journal of Counseling and Development,* 80 (1), 86–93.
www.assistedsuicide.org

What is the Future for Couple Counselling?

The UK's National Marriage Guidance Council (NMGC) was founded in 1938 in recognition of the problems facing married couples. At that time the model of lifelong heterosexual monogamy prevailed alongside Christian values and divorce was regarded as a dreadful, stigmatic event. Also at that time women had relatively little economic power and scant choice about 'staying or leaving', the contraceptive pill had not been invented, abortion was deeply shameful, the 'sexual revolution' had not happened (guilt and negative myths about masturbation still prevailed and little was said about the clitoral orgasm) and the typical family was only beginning to decline from several children towards three or two. Life expectancy also coloured expectations of a marriage but is now approaching an average of nearly 80 and is predicted to keep rising.

Clearly things were changing and are still changing, and the NMGC recognized these factors in its name change to Relate in 1988.

We now live in multicultural societies in which, like it or not, monogamy is not the only form of marriage or similar relationship, gay relationships can be honoured in civic ceremonies, teenage pregnancy and abortion are common, condom use is both common and openly promoted, and divorce is relatively easy and non-stigmatic. Many individuals do not enter committed relationships or marriages until their thirties, serial monogamy is common, single person households are common and single parenting is common. Unmarried cohabitation is no longer viewed as 'living in sin' but normal. Another huge shift since the 1930s is that often both parents will now work and families, while often financially better off, are 'time poor' and under stress. We commonly refer to our 'significant others' not as wives and husbands but as partners. About 45 per cent of marriages now end in divorce, frequently with a great deal of heartache, economic and family problems ensuing.

The ideal marriage – commencing in both partners falling in love, marrying and having children, raising their family and then remaining together 'till death us do part' – still, however, exerts a great pull on our expectations of ourselves. While the stigma of divorce or singledom has largely gone, there may still be a sense of failure for many in comparing themselves to couples who do apparently measure up to the ideal. Some research and folklore have concurred that the initial stage of starry-eyed romantic love and energetic, frequent sex lasts no longer than around three years. After that, couples must work at their relationship and couple counselling is part of this work. The common sources of disaffection with a partner are thought to be infidelity, sexual incompatibility, asymmetrical input (he does no housework), communication problems, conflicts about money and childrearing, parenting itself, growing apart and having nothing in common, and 'unreasonable behaviour'.

Couple counsellors, marital psychotherapists or relationship therapists often examine the attachment patterns of each partner, sometimes the relationship dynamics of their families of origin, communication between the partners and sexual and intimate behaviours. Couple counsellors have talked about 'the relationship as the client' and worked with the couple as a system, rather than with the two individuals. Feminism has contributed to our understanding of relationship dynamics and in popular culture there is much talk and literature about the differences between women and men. The remit of couple counsellors is now not necessarily to 'save the marriage' but where necessary to salvage civil relations and facilitate a separation.

Today, infidelity or longstanding relationships often originate on the internet. Some people are willing to experiment with swinging (free sex with others with their partners also present and sexually active), some experiment with or commit to a lifestyle of polyamory (non-possessive partnerships with two or more people), some are openly bisexual, transsexual, transvestite or committed to sadomasochistic practices. Viagra is extending men's sex lives and some women provided with reproductive assistance have given birth above 60. Work is even underway to develop highly responsive robots as intimate partners. Things are not quite what they were 70 years or so ago. There may be more promiscuous sex and higher divorce rates but there is also less hypocrisy, less suffering in silence and probably more satisfaction in sex. For many, there is no God, or there are competing gods with apparently different expectations for close relationships. Many of us find it difficult to envisage an exclusive relationship enduring for 30, 40, 50 years or longer. It is also recognized that perhaps 1 per cent of the population is altogether asexual and asocial.

It seems unlikely that we will return to yesterday's ideal of decades-long marriage for all but doubts, conflicts and heartache will probably remain. Couple counselling has already adjusted its theory and practice in line with cultural changes. The question remains as to whether couple counsellors can suspend their own and any cultural biases in favour of purely client-centred moral views and goals. Clients' value bases can range from extreme religious orthodoxy to extreme liberalism. The selection of trainees already focuses on client-centredness and non-judgementalism. Training will need to take in continuing cultural changes as well as personal awareness and sociological scholarship. We might also consider stronger links with education, teaching more on the nature of relationships, imparting resilience and interpersonal problem-solving skills. In a Reichian vision, couple counsellors might grapple with the question of an optimal sexual freedom and minimal jealousy. Family ethics demands that we consider the long-term good of children, loneliness in old age and other factors. In terms of links with futurology, increasing genetic knowledge and technological capacity may well radically alter the nature of marriage-type relationships. We might be genetically modified and internationally matched, for example. In the meantime research suggests that those receiving couple counselling do better than those who do not, although this finding cannot tell us whether those who sought counselling were better motivated to improve their relationship anyway.

Further reading

Kipnis, L. (1993) *Against Love: A Polemic.* New York: Pantheon.
Lano, K. & Parry, C. (1995) *Breaking the Barriers to Desire: New Approaches to Multiple Relationships.* Nottingham: Five Leaves.

57

Why has Counselling had So Many Detractors?

On the face of it one might think that an activity like counselling that seeks to address distress and help people feel and function better would be welcomed as nothing but a good thing. But we know that it has taken decades for it to be reasonably well accepted and even now it is not fully accepted. I include here the fact that psychoanalysis and psychotherapy have also had their detractors and critics. I shall now outline what I think have been the main criticisms:

1   Early impressions of psychoanalysis largely in the media made it seem a mysterious, indulgent, meandering process, possibly a con, conducted by an eccentric analyst who probably had more problems than others. Theories seemingly suggesting that you unconsciously wanted sex with your own mother were to be ridiculed or feared. Perhaps these images, however distorted, have never quite been shaken off.

2   In the UK there was some scepticism about a social practice that seemed very American – self-indulgent, touchy-feely (at least in its Californian guise), over-emotional, aimed at the gullible and affluent, and threatening to

challenge taboos. Therapy was probably conflated with encounter groups, nude marathons and the counterculture of drugs and uninhibited sex.

3   For some, it made no intuitive sense that some illnesses might be 'psychosomatic', that people were somehow imagining they had problems or inventing one problem to cover up another. It made them feel guilty about even being ill.

4   The long time many spent in therapy aroused the suspicion that it was a never-ending, self-perpetuating and expensive process that didn't really resolve anything.

5   When psychologists began to get involved and applied scientific principles of empirical research, it was realized that little or no hard evidence existed for therapy, that its claims to success were self-promoted case studies that no-one could independently verify. For some time therapists felt affronted and rejected such demands before finally having to engage in empirical, controlled research.

6   With the twentieth-century growth of hundreds of different, competing models of therapy, perhaps there was a sense not only of theoretical mayhem (any new idea is as good as another, anyone can create a new therapy) but also of unprincipled, guru-like chasers of money and reputation.

7   Gradually some stories began to emerge of charismatic and abusive therapists who had slept with patients/clients, exploited them and failed to deliver results. A small but steady stream of allegations and client publications over the years has added to such suspicions.

8   The expansion and gradual acceptance of counselling in the UK, in the voluntary sector, colleges and universities, commercial corporations, and the NHS, has also fuelled a suspicion that anyone with minimal training can become a counsellor. Objections that training is rigorous, demanding and overseen by the BACP and others cuts no ice with those who observe quite thinly educated people being accepted onto the increasing number of counselling training courses. The witnessing of so many trainees also disguises the fact that many of them probably have quite poor job prospects, since employment in counselling is more aspirational than solid.

9   The sometimes outlandish claims of therapists alongside a paucity of visibly impressive outcomes came to be contrasted with the relatively fast results coming to be seen in the use of pharmacological interventions, such as anti-depressants for depression. Genetic research too seems to move faster and much more impressively than counselling research, sometimes seriously challenging views about the origins of certain psychological and behavioural problems.

10   The eagerness of counsellors to get involved in the aftermath of large-scale disasters and personal traumas led to a perception among some of counsellors as distastefully opportunistic 'ambulance-chasers'.

11   The failure among counsellors, counselling psychologists, psychotherapists, psychoanalysts and some psychiatrists and other mental health

workers to agree on the place, purpose and aims of the hundreds of different models and who is best equipped to deliver services has led to some doubts about the possibilities for disciplined professionalization by statutory regulation.

12   The costs of counselling in both the private sector and the NHS, when considered in economically challenged times and compared with other health demands, become a serious concern. Rising population levels and increasing longevity also create questions about the economic limits for counselling applications.

It is possible, indeed even likely, that some of the negative criticism directed at counselling has arisen from the insecurities of attackers. It's been suggested, for example, that many journalists – themselves quite cynical, exposed to more than their share of worldly horrors and not always averse to alcoholic self-medicating behaviour – will attack as a means of defence. Counselling being portrayed as over-emotional may well be interpreted as a projective mechanism by a society in denial of its suppressed emotional needs. Britons however have probably become more sexually liberated across the last few decades and perhaps also more open emotionally, with the cathartic reaction to the death of Princess Diana in 1997 being claimed as a watershed moment.

In spite of many negative views spanning many decades, counselling has weathered the criticism and even apparently thrived, being accepted fairly extensively into the NHS and by the British public. The stiff upper lip culture has changed, research has produced some reassurance, GPs quite routinely refer patients to counsellors, and word of mouth about successful outcomes or helpfulness presumably also plays a part. The BACP, UKCP and others have sharpened voluntary regulation and complaints procedures and strongly encouraged further research. Currently, the 'counselling *vs* CBT' battle (most evident in IAPTs) still quietly rages and only time will tell how counselling will weather that challenge. In the dynamic ecology of social, economic and environmental forces, it will be interesting to see how counselling fares in the years to come.

Further reading

Dryden, W. & Feltham, C. (eds) (1992) *Psychotherapy and its Discontents*. Milton Keynes: Open University Press.
Feltham, C. (1999) Facing, understanding and learning from critiques of psychotherapy and counselling. *British Journal of Guidance and Counselling*, 27 (3), 301–312.
Masson, J.M. (1989) *Against Therapy*. London: Fontana.

58

To what Extent is Counselling
Reliant on Illusions?

We may not agree on what an illusion is. Let's say that a placebo pill produces an illusion of wellbeing, or at least the illusion that an effective ingredient is being ingested, which sometimes triggers a positive psychological effect. Unless we believe in magic, the positive effect depends not on any physical cause but on expectation alone. There are scientific and ethical problems with this but few would argue that the beneficial result isn't real and to be welcomed. So we can surely argue that harmless illusions in counselling leading to positive outcomes or enhanced client expectations must be a good thing. So what illusions are we talking about, exactly, and do we agree that they are illusions, and harmless?

First, consider the mystery and opaqueness of theoretical terminology and explanations. Clients are advised to elicit some such explanation. What is the counsellor's theoretical orientation? How exactly do the ingredients and techniques of this theory work? Many names of theoretical orientations are hyphenated or multi-worded (person-centred counselling, cognitive behaviour therapy, neurolinguistic programming, etc.), which may in itself impress or bewilder clients. It may make them disinclined to question further, and to take it on faith that the counselling and counsellor will be quite complex or clever. Some critics might indeed argue that the very need for polysyllabic terminology in this field is an act of obfuscation designed to bamboozle or create the illusion of special processes.

Every counsellor and psychotherapist will have some qualifications, many of them from a university or college, and often displayed on the wall of the counselling or consulting room. Almost all will have professional body endorsements.

These reinforce clients' faith that something therapeutic must be happening. The practitioner has studied, is endorsed and accountable. The room designated for counselling may be purpose-designed, or a room in a private house, or a clinic, but in all cases it will be set aside for counselling and quiet, private and conducive to reflection. In some cases rooms will be dimmed or decorated with environmental cues such as emotive pictures and technical books. An illusion of wisdom may be created. The seating arrangements and 'unnatural' attentiveness of the practitioner may help to enhance expectations of 'other-worldliness', psychological seriousness, intensity, exclusive attention, special-ness and confidentiality. Where else in our everyday lives do we receive such exclusive, one-way attention and interest, where our every word is hung upon and believed?

One of the most potent instruments of counselling is the asymmetry – that is, the counsellor listening intently and expecting nothing personal in return. Alongside this, there is counsellor non-self-disclosure (sometimes called abstinence in psychoanalysis). While practice differs somewhat across orientations, most counsellors will refrain from sharing their own personal information. There are good reasons for this but an illusion easily created thereby is that the counsellor is someone who has few or no problems. He or she has worked through their problems and obstacles, perhaps heroically, or transcended them. In any case, many clients will imagine that their counsellor is a model of coping or resilience. Whether or not this is explained in terms of transference, it is understandable that the asymmetrical conversation of counselling and the removal of information about the personal life of the counsellor should lead to an illusion that all is well in his or her life: 'If I work hard, disclose heroically and emote freely, I may attain the state of calm and wisdom of the counsellor', runs the fantasy of many clients. In addition, since most private practices are probably conducted in smart middle-class homes (in the counselling rooms of which an air of special order and tidiness may prevail for public relations reasons), the client may wish or fantasize that her efforts might or should result in similar affluence, calm and poise. How many private practices are run from untidy rooms in dilapidated houses in poor neighbourhoods?

Now, the counsellor in the above position may in fact be a well-rounded person living in an atmosphere of success and calm, and I am obviously not advocating that counsellors ignore all such matters, present themselves in a dishevelled manner and freely and symmetrically self-disclose. But I suggest that these environmental and presentational features create and strengthen illusions that lie at the core of counselling practice. If the client is 'compliant', accepts the theoretical explanation offered and buys into the fantasy of the counsellor as a fully-functional, almost superhuman person, this may well boost both therapeutic commitment and success. But can solid personal growth rest on a foundation of illusions?

Further reading

Epstein, W. (1995) *The Illusion of Psychotherapy*. Edison, NJ: Transaction.
Frank, J.D. (1974) *Persuasion and Healing: A Comparative Study of Psychotherapy*. New York: Shocken.
Fromm, E. (1980) *Beyond the Chains of Illusion*. London: Abacus.
Taylor, S.E. (1991) *Positive Illusions: Creative Self-Deception and the Healthy Mind*. New York: Basic Books.

59

Who is the 'Person of Tomorrow'?

Carl Rogers posited the image of the person of tomorrow who would, by therapy or other personal growth means, transcend most of today's suboptimal character traits. Rogers alluded to people being 'young in mind', 'interested in a simpler life', 'assertive and positive', 'freer, richer, more self-directed'. They would show openness, authenticity, a 'scepticism regarding science and technology', intimacy, caring, a closeness to nature, an anti-institutional attitude, an indifference to material comforts. This view comes from one man, an American, in the 1970s. Some have called the humanistic approaches romantic and Rogers' views naïve. But it is interesting that few writers in this field have much to say about visions of the future human being.

To some extent Rogers was always reacting against authority but he and his contemporaries were also reacting to an ever-present threat of world war and nuclear proliferation, and a consolidating materialism. Today's world (in a new millennium) seems to have hardened into an acceptance of technology and materialism, as well as the continuing realities and possibilities of war. We also have the threat of climate change. There are signs of greater tolerance (the gradual erosion of racism and homophobia, for example) but I am less sure about a growth in 'humanness'. While some people have opted for a simpler lifestyle (giving up stressful well-paid jobs for a downshifted lifestyle, growing their own vegetables, etc.) a majority probably remain locked in somewhat stressful lifestyles. Many couples with children somehow hold down two jobs. Many of us are hooked on consumerism, for example on multiple cheap holidays, high mortgages, property and other investments to enrich us. Overall it isn't the picture that Rogers seemed to have in mind.

Step back for a moment to ask whether (a) it is the task of counsellors and their professional bodies to envisage the future, and if (b) any particular vision of the future fits well with the counselling ethos. We might say that counselling is pragmatic and short term, concerned only with the current wellbeing of the client presenting for counselling, and that counselling in all its theoretical variety cannot favour any vision of the future or image of the person of tomorrow. Paradoxically counselling works towards reducing mental health problems or problems in living so that, were it to work extremely well and extensively, there would be less and less need for it. The BACP's vision of an 'emotionally healthy society' doesn't really acknowledge the obstacles in store, however, one of which is a lack of agreement on possibilities, goals and means.

So, if any of us considers what our ideal image of a person of tomorrow is, what is it? Don't diversity and individuality stand in the way of any *one* image? Feminists would presumably envisage men of tomorrow who are caring, communicative, empathic and genuinely egalitarian, yet others might want to stress independence, resilience and resourcefulness as the primary desirable qualities and values. These need not be mutually exclusive but could easily become so. CBT practitioners would presumably wish to envisage future humans as highly rational and stoical, while Gestalt thinkers might emphasize responsibility, dialogue and authenticity, and psychosynthesis practitioners would probably place a very high value on spirituality. Psychodynamic thinkers would value better childrearing practices and a more insightful consciousness of inner processes, while solution-focused thinkers would stress the immediate building of personal strengths and constructive behaviours. Few of these would have much to say about social realities, about education, politics, or the environment.

Shift now to a consideration of other groups in society concerned with tomorrow and the person of tomorrow. Most would agree that humans have problems and do not reach their full potential. But many – sometimes referred to as transhumanists or posthumanists – want to enhance intelligence, for example, by means of neurological improvements and closer technological link-ups. In other words, their envisaged task is to reduce our cognitive faults so that we work more like creative machines and in co-operation with digital technology. Others see ageing and death as the greatest human flaws (bio-engineering problems) and are working on radical improvements, some even envisioning a human lifespan of up to 1,000 years. Some are working on space travel. While they may factor in the emotional and economic consequences and so on, their main focus seems to be on creating a kind of superhuman. Nor are they apparently opposed to a capitalist, consumerist culture and continuing economic growth, but see the future in optimistic, hedonistic terms. Against this vision, humanistic therapy visions look decidedly romantic. Is our 'humanness' best enhanced by co-operating with science and technology (not what Rogers had in mind) or in a more anarchistic, back-to-nature vision? We probably can't have it all ways. We may also have to accept that each generation will face different realities and hold different values.

Further reading

Garreau, J. (2005) *Radical Evolution*. New York: Broadway.
Greenfield, S. (2003) *Tomorrow's People: How 21st Century Technology is Changing the Way We Think and Feel*. London: Allen Lane.
Rogers, C. (1980) *A Way of Being*. Boston, MA: Houghton Mifflin.

What does the Writer Really Think?

So-called scientific texts, incluing the psychological, are traditionally composed without the 'I' of the author of being visible. This cumbersome convention serves the purpose of making the text appear objective. Obviously an 'I' appearing in any paper shows that a particular, fallible human being has written it, and that person may well be importing subjective views into it. In counselling training, writing in the first person is often required, especially in more personal assignments but also more generally. This is not to substitute non-rigorous, sloppy writing for a formal evidenced style but resonates with the postmodernist critique of traditional academic writing as pretending it has the 'view from nowhere'. Instead, the voice of the author and her or his situatedness is openly included. There is an attempt to avoid the tradition of presenting subjective (and mixed) views that masquerade as objective scientific evidence.

I have made various references to my own views along the way in this book and I now want to be as open as I can be, if briefly, about my own situation and views. I am a white heterosexual male, an atheist, 59 years old at the time of writing, and these identities probably colour my writing. I have been involved in personal growth projects for about 35 years, including an engagement in Janov's primal therapy in Los Angeles in 1978–79. I think I have moved from a position of sympathy with radical humanistic therapy to a mixed approach (transtheoretical) and also some scepticism. I have had primal therapy, some psychoanalytic psychotherapy, person-centred counselling and couple counselling. None of these have been unqualified successes but I've taken something from each, most powerfully from primal therapy. I trained in counselling at Aston University in 1980 with Windy Dryden and Richard Nelson-Jones and picked up some knowledge of and respect for aspects of rational emotive behaviour therapy. I have worked in a variety of settings, including probation, mental health, alcoholism treatment, an employee assistance programme, a university counselling service and in private practice.

As a full-time academic I found it increasingly difficult to continue in counselling practice (for lack of time) and often felt fraudulent about this. But I have remained a supervisor and trainer and have studied and written on many counselling topics. I think I have always had a sceptical and icono-clastic temperament, which leads me to wonder to what extent this may be a personality trait for some people, and whether critical thinking may or may not be easily taught. I am also aware that critical thinking and free speech are not fully vouchsafed to any of us, and tutors, employers, professional bodies and publishers often (presumably unintentionally) constrain us. It is not unusual, either, to be unfairly condemned as 'cynical' when raising objections to conventional positive thinking. Critics of this 'anti-critical' kind would do well to reflect on the true meaning of cynicism in ancient Greek thought, including its attack on *typhos,* or popular clichés and learned obfuscation, often by means of *parrhesia,* or 'speaking truth to power' (Desmond, 2008).

In 2004 I had a book published called *Problems Are Us, Or Is It Just Me?* It proved impossible to find a mainstream publisher and I made no money from the book but received very good feedback from those who read it. While I looked at the nature of human problems generally, I also made copious use of my own life experiences as illustrations. My intention was partly to be as honest and transparent as possible but also to make the point that most, if not all of us, suffer from all sorts of problems but are wary of talking about them and often hide them. At least, some people will try to hide their problems, even from themselves, and this can make them even sicker. Many of our problems may be of a subtle genetic origin in my view, and many have socio-economic roots; some are self-made and self-perpetuated but many are not, and may not be modi-fiable. We need not feel guilty about that. But if we are going to continue living (and life doesn't always feel pleasurable or worthwhile) we need to find ways to endure.

Given my many critical publications, I have naturally been asked what I really think about counselling, as if to criticize is to condemn totally. I think we can value something without *over*-valuing it. I have not found therapies claiming to effect dramatic personal changes credible. But I believe that in this very often brutal world individuals can use all the help available. Many good-hearted, perceptive people are offering a listening and talking therapy that restores others' humanity and ability to cope. Therefore I continue to find counselling and psychotherapy worthwhile and interesting but not all of their theories and claims meaningful or helpful. In some ways I would like to see a down to earth, commonsense, generic model of psychological therapy used in training, with counsellors being free to indulge their theoretical preferences later. I would like to see counselling more freely available but delivered humanly with as little professional paraphernalia and bureaucracy as possible. At its best, unpretentious counselling remains one of the few arenas today in which humanness is preserved and promoted.

My *What's Wrong With Us? The Anthropathology Thesis* (Feltham, 2007) expanded on my exploration of why human beings may have gone astray historically and remain dysfunctional. This is not a popular view among most counsellors because it contains strong elements of determinism, negativity and pessimism; and it speaks of 'us' rather than only the 'I' of counselling tradition. It also challenges many of the claims made by counselling theory and by the professional bodies. There is a certain risk in taking up highly critical positions but I believe that radical honesty is, as Blanton (1994) argues, necessary for mental health, and free speech is necessary for a healthy society (Appignanesi, 2005). In my view it would be regrettable if counselling and psychotherapy ever hardened into an orthodoxy whose over-sensitive defenders prevented others from voicing their sincere reservations freely, and from making recommendations for change.

Further reading

Appignanesi, L. (ed.) (2005) *Free Expression is No Offence.* London: Penguin.

Blanton, B. (1994) *Radical Honesty.* New York: Dell.

Desmond, W. (2008) *Cynics.* Stocksfield: Acumen.

Feltham, C. (2007) *What's Wrong With Us? The Anthropathology Thesis.* Chichester: Wiley.

Perennial and Current Topics:

Challenge

Some subjects have been debated for decades and not resolved, such as the place of emotion and science in counselling. We are now in a position, with counselling being quite well established in the UK, of being able to silence many critics by sheer survival, but is this a good thing? Does the simple endurance of a movement like counselling ensure that it is 'truthful' and 'immortal'? To what extent might changing social conditions and ethics (for example, the assisted dying debate or the changing nature of relationships) alter any core values and practices in counselling? It is inevitable that counselling innovators will track social changes and respond with new theory and practice. Like the author, when you honestly reflect on what you really think, where are you situated, and what part do you find that subjectivity plays in your views and practice?

Case Study

Vicky is a university lecturer who sits on a research committee of her professional body. She has some modest opportunities to influence policy. She is aware that certain topics for research are fashionable and expedient, that government funding is likely to support certain lines of enquiry and that some professional agendas will be better served by promoting matters of effectiveness and quality control. On the other hand, some of her own students are researching quite challenging new areas and she herself is interested in some unconventional avenues of enquiry. Vicky is frustrated by many research policy decisions. She deals with this by writing speculatively and sceptically on themes of intuition, suicide and counselling-related social trends but this earns her little respect in her university and her promotion prospects are limited unless she can raise research funds. How far do you think professional directions are so influenced? Does a hierarchy of respect exist, with funded empirical research on top, 'soft research' lower down and speculative and critical thinking somewhere near the bottom? How would you judge some research questions to be more important or trivial than others? (See Heaton, 1993.)

Critical thinking perspectives

Vicky could as she sees it 'sell out', secure funds for a major research project in an area of enquiry that is fashionable and government-approved, which would gain her a research assistant, add to her research profile and might help her get promoted. On the other hand she might decide to interview a small number of colleagues and students informally in order to discover quite directly more about attitudes to suicide and assisted dying. Instead of pursuing scholarly glory and promotion she might write about her interests journalistically, join organizations like Dignity in Dying and/or create her own networks of like-minded people for discussion and political activism. Rather than clinging to the pose of academic objectivity she might 'come out' as strongly in favour of rational suicide and assisted dying.

Appendices

Appendix 1

Sample of Critical Textual Analysis

Below, you will find a passage on supervision. It is not an actual passage but one I have constructed (and the reference is fictitious) but in some respects it contains some typical claims and arguments. I have of course deliberately exaggerated and distorted in places for demonstration purposes. Read through it and – using what natural critical thinking skills you have – identify its errors and raise any questions that can be asked about it. My own suggested questions in relation to this passage are found below.

All right-minded therapists are aware that counselling supervision is essential. The BACP has made it clear that it is unethical to practise without supervision. Supervision mirrors the intense relationship between client and counsellor and ensures that practice remains safe and excellent. McSmith and O'Dear's (1984) research showed conclusively not only that counsellors value supervision highly but also that without it clinical errors would multiply and clients would be abused. Supervision is the jewel in the crown of the counselling profession and it seems suspicious that anyone would oppose it, especially those in the profession who should know better. It is likely that critics of supervision fail to understand the power of parallel process. There is also a danger that they may undermine the profession. Supervision, as has been stated, is essential and should be fully funded. Also, more research is urgently needed into the processes underpinning supervision and in order to identify best methods, best timing and best training. Without this, the mental health of the nation is at risk.

McSmith, A. & O'Dear, O. (1984) Counselling supervision: a qualitative study of supervisors' experiences and beliefs. *Journal of Advanced Counselling*, 3 (2), 101–103.

Appendix 1: Analysis

1   A phrase like 'right-minded' is loaded and precludes further enquiry. 'All' also implies a consensus.

2   'Essential' does not tell us what it is essential for, nor is there any discussion here about what supervision is or what its allegedly essential ingredients are.

3   Using 'has made it clear' and 'unethical to practise' shuts down enquiry. Citing a single professional body as a final authority may tend to shut down enquiry. Is it in fact strictly *unethical* or, rather, poor practice according to one view? How and by whom was that view and policy arrived at with no research to support it?

4   Is the client–counsellor relationship always intense and is supervision necessarily similarly intense? Might this hold some truth for certain theoretical approaches but not for others?

5   Can supervision really ensure safety (and what is safety)? 'Excellence' is a very vague term and cannot be ensured.

6   The research cited is quite dated and extremely unlikely to be conclusive, especially at three pages long (but if it were conclusive, why would further research be needed?) and presumably it cannot show that *all* counsellors value supervision unless all were consulted. 'Value' is a vague and loaded term. A piece of such research could not say what *would* happen without supervision (or with it) and 'errors' and 'abused' are speculative and scare-mongering, emotive terms. These also suggest that supervision prevents client abuse, a claim for which we have no evidence.

7   'Jewel in the crown' is a somewhat romantic metaphor and it is possible that not everyone would agree with this uncritical assertion.

8   'Suspicious' and 'should know better' emotively suggest that anyone who queries any aspect of supervision is perhaps deviant, naughty or immature. This is a sly, combined projection of an offence, and a telling off. 'Oppose it' implies that scrutiny is taboo, and any criticism is a kind of inadmissible disloyalty rather than a human right to freedom of thought and expression.

9   'It is likely' really means here 'in my opinion', and 'fail to understand' appears in place of 'do not agree with the idea of'. Parallel process is a psychodynamic concept and not everyone accepts it is a reality, or as powerful or important.

10   The danger of undermining the profession is an emotive point and a vague 'hands off' warning: the profession must be supported at all times and critics should be wary.

11   To repeat 'supervision is essential' does not make this claim any clearer or truer, and the link with funding (by whom and for what?) is tenuous and emotive.

12   Exactly what underpinning supervision processes are being alluded to here and what makes such research so urgent? By this point in the passage it has been assumed that supervision is essential and that it performs certain functions. This (and the BACP mandate) mean that certain aspects

of supervision simply cannot be researched. You could not have a control group of unsupervised counsellors, for example.

13   The point about the mental health of the nation demonstrates an absurdity about the sense of proportion, of course. Few writers would make such a statement but some probably (in my opinion) exaggerate the importance of supervision in the scheme of things.

14   This passage combines an appeal to emotions and to the authority of a professional body. It doesn't allow for subtleties of enquiry and it makes the assumption that 'research' will provide the solution for any gap in knowledge. It is assumed that research *will* validate supervision: what would happen if it didn't? Is it conceivable that BACP would abandon its mandatory supervision policy if research failed to validate it?

15   Critiques of supervision are dismissed here as somewhat dangerous, disloyal and childish. While the familiar call for 'more research' is made, no allowance for philosophical analysis or critical thinking is made.

16   Critics of statutory regulation have pointed out that their well-articulated arguments have been dealt with by simply being ignored or marginalized. Might it be that vested interests in supervision operate similarly, that is by calling for (inconclusive and extremely slow) research, but tacitly ignoring inconvenient critical thinking? In other words, it may not matter what you have to say critically about supervision because we are going to continue to do what we've always done anyway.

17   How can we separate out writings about counselling that are purely subjective, emotive, openly persuasive, based on 'practice wisdom', logical, based on empirical research or leading to research, or of a purely public relations kind? Should writers always try to declare their otherwise covert interests (e.g. to maintain the supervision tradition, to protect my livelihood, to publicize myself, to get funding, to attack someone)? How can a fair balance and transparency be achieved?

18   In what ways in this slightly spoof passage might I (CF) have smuggled in my own agenda and views on supervision? In what ways might I be trying subtly to persuade you to think like me? And what is it in you that leans towards or against my perspective?

19   What would be the effect of reading all texts in this quite detailed critical way? (See as a guide Wodak, R. & Meyer, M. (2001) *Methods of Critical Discourse Analysis*. London: Sage.) Might it not lead to tedium and paralysis? Must some things be taken on trust?

20   Are there any justified limits to critical thinking? For example, would it be warranted in principle to critique all the claims regarding counselling supervision to the point of coming to reject it as spurious or unproven, or as part of an agenda of authoritarian professional control? What happens when critical thinking finds itself up against a brick wall? Also, since it's possible that a kind of defensive, untrusting, pathological character trait manifests itself in always opposing authority and asking endless questions, how can we distinguish this from legitimate and useful critical thinking?

Appendix 2

Some Critical Thinking Matters in Therapeutic Practice

Critical decisions and questions in professional life and training

Shall I undertake counselling/therapy training? Am I suitable?

Shall I re-mortgage my house in order to pay my considerable course fees?

Have I chosen the right course for myself (e.g. the most compatible theoretical model)? Can I change if I want to?

How will I accommodate, afford and react to my training therapy?

How is this training going to impact on my family?

If I don't agree with my tutor/s, is it OK to voice this?

How do I decide on any specialisms, further training, employment or private practice?

Which criteria should I use to choose a supervisor?

Should I retain links with my existing profession in case I don't find sufficient work as a therapist?

How will I deal with any conflicts between myself as a practitioner and my managers and organization?

Critical thinking at assessment

What processes are necessary as regards self-referral, telephone enquiries, screening and allocation to practitioners?

To what extent do I use any notes provided about my new client?

Do I have a good grasp of this client's concerns?

Am I competent to work with her?

If I have not worked with this kind of presenting concern before, are there any risks I should take into account?

How transparent should I be with this potential client about my experience or relative lack of experience with her concerns?

What critical issues exist regarding my theoretical orientation, this person's presenting concerns, NICE guidelines, etc.?

Can this person's concerns be substantially resolved within my service's time limits, if they have these?

Is this person ready, motivated and robust enough for counselling or psychotherapy?

Am I aware of suitable referral links should they become necessary?

Are there any particular ethical concerns that arise with this client?

Critical in-session and between-session considerations

Are there any early warning signs of unhelpful friction in our relationship?

What transferential clues are apparent from the outset?

Am I getting any feelings of fear, dread, boredom, attraction or unusual insight-fulness with this client?

In what ways is this client challenging my usual style of doing therapy?

How confident or considered am I in varying my practice when it feels right, against principles I was taught?

What uncomfortable moments have there been?

What good moments and turning points have there been?

At which points have I drifted off, failed to grasp the client's point or felt stuck?

Am I feeling that I have to solve the client's problems?

Is there any sense of not believing, or finding it hard to believe, the client?

Are there any ways in which my client and I are at odds, e.g. regarding expectations of the length and depth of therapy?

In what ways might I creatively and legitimately improvise interventions with this client?

Is it OK to practise eclectically based on strong hunches?

Should I use a technique I haven't used before or wait until after I have discussed it in supervision?

Are our personalities unhelpfully different in any ways?

Do any awkward frictions or unspoken matters exist, e.g. differences in class, race, culture, sexuality?

Is it difficult to tell my client that his problems seem too complex and/or non-psychological, for therapy to help as much as he hopes?

How can I tell my client that he is wandering, using small talk or being defensive?
If in private practice, will I honestly tell this client that I don't think he will benefit from further sessions?
How long do I think it's normal or acceptable for therapy to continue?
How do I feel if either I or the client mentions wanting to end and there being disagreement about this?
How detailed are my notes and how would I feel if my client wanted to see them?
Is it OK for my client to telephone me between sessions in some circumstances?
Do I find myself not talking much about this client in supervision, or bringing them up much more than others?

Critical questions about professional development

Should I retrain substantially in order to update myself or improve my employment options?
How often should I change my supervisor or supervision arrangements?
Should I cover my options by joining multiple professional bodies, or by leaving one to join another?
Given my limited budget for CPD, which workshops or conferences are best for me to attend?
To what extent will I read – and find useful – scholarly articles on empirical research?
What would I do if I found my views on practice in conflict with NICE guidelines?
What sense shall I make of discussions on statutory regulation?
Should I re-enter my own therapy?
How can I address my job stress?
If I sensed that I might be past my professional best as I get older, what would I do?
If I apply meta-critical thinking to my work (e.g. by reflecting on philosophical and sociological viewpoints on human distress) where might this take me?

Appendix 3

Additional Questions

Consider the following questions and what arguments you can think of to respond to them in positive and negative terms. Do you think any of these questions themselves are taboo or unhelpful? Consider also what additional questions you can think of – especially those which are important to you – and expand on these.

1   How useful or otherwise are questionnaires for clients?
2   Are there any circumstances at all in which friendly or sexual contact with a client might be permissible or even therapeutic?
3   Why are strong challenge and confrontation used relatively rarely in counselling and perhaps especially in statutory settings?
4   How can therapy lasting many years be justified?
5   Is there anything impractical or unethical about counselling that lasts for only six sessions?
6   Are certain aspects of human being or functioning neglected (e.g. the body)?
7   What is the 'self' and exactly what do we mean by 'therapist use of self'?
8   How important is it to understand causative factors in clients' problems?
9   Can theories of evolutionary psychology and evolutionary psychiatry add to our understanding of clients?
10   Will persistent evidence-seeking eventually marginalize or discredit certain approaches?
11   Are some therapeutic approaches more dubious or dangerous than others?
12   Is counselling primarily a middle-class activity?
13   Why do some countries have little or no counselling tradition?
14   What reality do birth trauma, therapeutic rebirth and spiritual rebirth have?
15   Are there really master practitioners?
16   Is it conceivable that counselling and psychotherapy will one day merge under one title?

17   What place do the exploration of dreams, subpersonalities and transpersonal phenomena have in counselling in short-term contracts in statutory settings?
18   How can we square the belief in repressed memories with involuntary traumatic memories?
19   Should counselling training be audited and reduced commensurate with employment opportunities?
20   Is there any evidence that accredited counsellors are more effective than unaccredited counsellors?
21   Should counsellors be installed in all schools?
22   How realistic is it for counsellors in specialist counselling agencies (e.g. alcohol, eating disorders, bereavement) to confine clients to working on presenting concerns?
23   Should we consider limiting counselling practice to counsellors of a certain age (e.g. 25–65)?
24   Should it be compulsory for counselling trainers to remain in practice alongside their academic responsibilities?
25   Do counsellors tend to 'over-psychologize' clients' concerns?
26   To what extent is it practical for counselling to address needs for childcare, interpreters and other forms of assistance?
27   Would money spent on research and a professional infrastructure be better spent on providing counselling services?
28   If it were possible to arrange for highly intensive experiential research into profound personality transformation in the direction of reduced neuroticism and narcissism and enhanced pro-sociality and eco-consciousness, would this be desirable?
29   Given the profile of an ageing population, should the government fund research into counselling needs for older people?
30   If genetic, neurological, pharmacological and cybernetic advances were to promise more assured improvements than the talking therapies, would counselling disappear?

Now add on any questions of your own.

References

BACP (2010) *Ethical Framework for Good Practice in Counselling and Psychotheraphy.* Lutterworth: British Association for Counselling and Psychotherapy.

Barnett, R. (1997) *Higher Education: A Critical Business.* Buckingham: Open University Press.

Blanton, B. (1994) *Radical Honesty.* New York: Dell.

Brown, K. & Rutter, L. (2006) *Critical Thinking for Social Work.* Exeter: Learning Matters.

Charlton, B. (2000) *Psychiatry and the Human Condition.* Oxford: Radcliffe Medical Press.

Clare, A.W. & Thompson, S. (1981) *Let's Talk about Me.* London: BBC.

Cloud, D.L. (1998) *Control and Consolation in American Culture and Politics: Rhetoric of Therapy.* Thousand Oaks, CA: Sage.

Cottrell. S. (2005) *Critical Thinking Skills: Developing Effective Analysis and Argument.* London: Palgrave.

Crews, F. (ed.) (1999) *Unauthorised Freud: Doubters Confront a Legend.* New York: Penguin.

Cushman, P. (1996) *Constructing the Self, Constructing America: A Cultural History of Psychotherapy.* Cambridge, MA: Da Capo.

Dawes, R.M. (1996) *Psychology and Psychotherapy Built on Myth.* New York: Free Press.

Diedrich, L. (2005) A bioethics of failure: antiheroic cancer narrative. In M. Shildrick & R. Mykitiuk (eds), *Ethics of the Body: Postconventional Challenges.* Cambridge, MA: MIT Press.

Dryden, W. (ed.) (1992) *Hard-Earned Lessons from Counselling in Action.* London: Sage.

Dryden, W. & Feltham, C. (eds) (1992) *Psychotherapy and its Discontents.* Buckingham: Open University Press.

Du Gay, P. (2000) *In Praise of Bureaucracy.* London: Sage.

Elkins, J. (2001) *Why Art Cannot be Taught.* Champaign, IL: University of Illinois Press.

Ellenberger, H.F. (1971) *The Discovery of the Unconscious: The History and Evolution of Dynamic Psychiatry.* New York: Basic Books.

Erwin, E. (1997) *Philosophy and Psychotherapy.* London: Sage.

Eysenck, H.J. (1952) The effects of psychotherapy: an evaluation. *Journal of Consulting Psychology*, 16, 319–324.

Feltham, C. (2007) *What's Wrong With Us? The Anthropathology Thesis*. Chichester: Wiley.

Feltham, C. (1999a) Facing, understanding and learning from critiques of psychotherapy and counselling. *British Journal of Guidance and Counselling*, 27 (3), 301–312.

Feltham, C. (ed.) (1999b) *Controversies in Psychotherapy and Counselling*. London: Sage.

Feltham, C. (ed.) (1997) *Which Psychotherapy? Leading Exponents Explain their Differences*. London: Sage.

Feltham, C. (1995) *What is Counselling? The Promise and Problem of the Talking Therapies*. London: Sage.

Finke, R.A. & Bettle, J. (1996) *Chaotic Cognition: Principles and Applications*. Mahwah, NJ: Lawrence Erlbaum.

Fisher, A. (2001) *Critical Thinking: An Introduction*. Cambridge: Cambridge University Press.

Fox, D. & Prilleltensky, I. (eds) (1997) *Critical Psychology: An Introduction*. London: Sage.

Furedi, F. (2004) *Therapy Culture: Cultivating Vulnerability in an Uncertain Age*. London: Routledge.

Groopman, J. (2008) *How Doctors Think*. Boston, MA: Houghton Mifflin.

Heaton, J.M. (1993) The sceptical tradition in psychotherapy. In L. Spurling (ed.), *From the Words of My Mouth: Tradition in Psychotherapy*. London: Routledge.

Heyward, C. (1993) *When Boundaries Betray Us: Beyond Illusions of What is Ethical in Therapy and Life*. San Francisco, CA: HarperCollins.

Hillman, J. & Ventura, M. (1992) *We've Had a Hundred Years of Psychotherapy and the World's Getting Worse*. San Francisco, CA: Harper.

Holmes, G. (2002) What is called thinking? *The Journal of Critical Psychology, Counselling and Psychotherapy*, 2 (1), 33–39.

House, R. (2003) *Therapy Beyond Modernity: Deconstructing and Transcending Profession-Centred Therapy*. London: Karnac.

House, R. & Loewenthal, D. (eds) (2008) *Against and For CBT: Towards a Constructive Dialogue?* Ross-on-Wye: PCCS Books.

Howard, A. (1996) *Challenges to Counselling and Psychotherapy*. Basingstoke: Palgrave.

Jackins, H. (1978) *The Upward Trend*. Seattle, WA: Rational Island Press.

Jacobs, M. (2000) *Illusion: A Psychodynamic Interpretation of Thinking and Belief*. London: Whurr.

Kirschner, S.R. (1996) *The Religious and Romantic Origins of Psychoanalysis: Individuation and Integration in Post-Freudian Theory*. Cambridge: Cambridge University Press.

Kottler, J. (2002) *Bad Therapy: Master Therapists Share Their Worst Failures*. London: Routledge.

Lambert, M.J. (1992) Psychotherapy outcome research: implications for integrative and eclectic therapists. In J.C. Norcross & M.R. Goldfried (eds), *Handbook of Psychotherapy Integration*. New York: Basic Books.

Lavery, K.T. (2007) *The Maturity of Belief: Critically Assessing Religious Faith*. London: Continuum.

Lawton, B. & Feltham, C. (eds) (2000) *Taking Supervision Forward: Enquiries and Trends*. London: Sage.

Loewenthal, D. (2003) *Post-modernism for Psychotherapists: A Critical Reader*. London: Brunner-Routledge.

Lomas, P. (1993) *Cultivating Intuition: An Introduction to Psychotherapy*. Northvale, NJ: Aronson.

Lynch, A. (1996) *Thought Contagion: How Belief Spreads Through Society*. New York: Basic Books.

Nelson-Jones, R. (1989) *Effective Thinking Skills*. London: Cassell.

Newman, F. (2003) Undecidable emotions (What is social therapy? And how is it revolutionary?). *Journal of Constructivist Psychology,* 16, 215–232.

NIMH (2009) The impact of mental illness on society. Available at www.nimh.nih.gov/health/topics/statistics/index.shtm/

Orlans, V. & Van Scoyoc, S. (2009) *A Short Introduction to Counselling Psychology*. London: Sage

Parker, I. (2007) *Revolution in Psychology: Alienation to Emancipation*. London: Pluto.

Parker, I. (ed.) (1999) *Deconstructing Psychotherapy*. London: Sage.

Pesut, D.J. & Herman, J. (1999) *Clinical Reasoning: The Art and Science of Critical and Creative Thinking*. New York: Delmar.

Pilgrim, D. (1997) *Psychotherapy and Society*. London: Sage.

Postle, D. (2007) *Regulating the Psychological Therapies: from Taxonomy to Taxidermy*. Ross-on-Wye: PCCS Books.

Robb, C. (2007) *This Changes Everything: The Relational Revolution in Psychology*. London: Picador.

Robertiello, R.C. & Schoenewolf, G. (1987) *101 Common Therapeutic Blunders: Countertransference and Counterresistance in Psychotherapy*. Northvale, NJ: Aronson.

Rose, N. (1989) *Governing the Soul: The Shaping of the Private Self*. London: Routledge.

Rosen, R.D. (1977) *Psychobabble: Fast Talk and Quick Cure in the Era of Feeling*. London: Wildwood House.

Safouan, M. (2000) *Jacques Lacan and the Question of Psychoanalytic Training*. Basingstoke: Macmillan.

Samuels, A. (1993) *The Political Psyche*. London: Routledge.

Sanders, P. (2005) Principled and strategic opposition to the medicalisation of distress and all of its apparatus. In S. Joseph & R. Worsley (eds), *Person-Centred Psychopathology: A Positive Psychology of Mental Health*. Ross-on-Wye: PCCS Books.

Schutz, W. (1979) *Profound Simplicity*. New York: Bantam.

Skovholt, T.M. & Ronnestad, M.H. (1995) *The Evolving Professional Self: Stages and Themes in Therapist and Counselor Development*. Chichester: Wiley.

Sloan, T. (ed.) (2000) *Critical Psychology: Voices for Change*. Basingstoke: Macmillan.

Smail, D. (2005) *Power, Interest and Psychology: Elements of a Social Materialist Understanding of Distress*. Ross-on-Wye: PCCS Books.

Spurling, L. (ed.) (1993) *From the Words of my Mouth: Tradition in Psychotherapy*. London: Routledge.

Szasz, T. (1976) *Anti-Freud: Karl Kraus's Criticism of Psychoanalysis and Psychiatry*. Syracuse: Syracuse University Press.

Weatherill, R. (2004) *Our Last Great Illusion: A Radical Psychoanalytical Critique of Therapy Culture*. Exeter: Imprint Academic.

Zweig, C. & Abrams, J. (eds) (1991) *Meeting the Shadow: The Hidden Power of the Dark Side of Human Nature*. New York: Tarcher.

Index

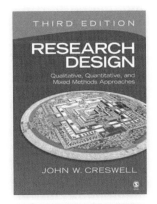
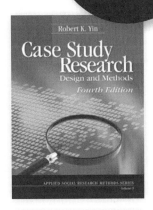

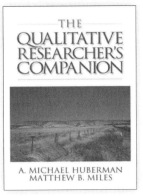
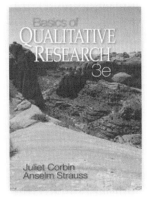

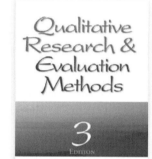
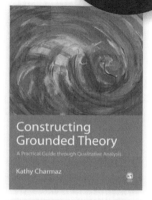

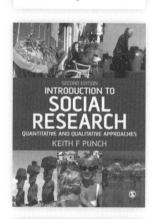
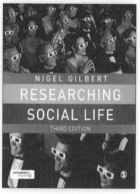
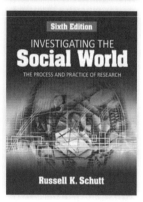